The man who would arrive at the doors of artistic creation with none of the madness of the Muses would be convinced that technical skill alone was enough to make an artist...what that man creates by means of reason alone will pale before the art of inspired beings.

- PLATO, PHÆDRUS, CA. 370 B.C.

Madness of the Muses

The Art of
Ingrid Dee Magidson

Edited by
Jay Magidson

Stratumentis Publishing
www.Stratumentis.com

for my family,
whose unconditional love
keeps me from floating away

Cover: *Gaia,* Layered Mixed Media, 2012 by Ingrid Dee Magidson
Book and Cover Design by Gessocat

July 2013 ISBN 13: 978-0-9840213-5-2 (Hardcover)

ART / Subjects & Themes / Portraits
ART / Individual Artists / Monographs
ART / Mixed Media

PRINTED IN CANADA

Stratumentis Publishing
www.Stratumentis.com

Contents

Looking Forward and Back
AN INTRODUCTION BY INGRID DEE MAGIDSON — 6

Madness of the Muses
AN INTRODUCTION BY JAY MAGIDSON — 16

Temptation
AN INTRODUCTION BY BRADLEY E. PLACE, JR. — 22

Past Becomes Present
STEWART OXENHORN, THE ASPEN TIMES — 26

ART SELECTIONS - 2007 — 28

ART SELECTIONS - 2008 — 38

ART SELECTIONS - 2009 — 56

ART SELECTIONS - 2010 — 68

ART SELECTIONS - 2011 — 88

ART SELECTIONS - 2012 — 102

Ingrid Dee Magidson - Incarnazioni
FEDERICA GALETTO, CENTRO SOCIALE DELL'ARTE — 104

ART SELECTIONS - 2013 — 120

Balancing a Family Life and a Creative Life
BRENDA HOPE ZAPPITELL, PROFESSIONAL ARTIST MAGAZINE — 122

CATALOGUE OF THE COMPLETE WORKS 2006 - 2013 — 138

CURRICULUM VITÆ (RÉSUMÉ) — 166

LIFE AND WORK - IN PHOTOS — 170

ACKNOWLEDGEMENTS — 176

Looking Forward and Back

An Introduction by Ingrid Dee Magidson

I WAS born an artist. It took me nearly 40 years to discover that. However, looking back, it all lines up in a pattern or design I couldn't have arranged better if I had planned it. I come from a family of artists. My father is a painter and sculptor and my mother is a fiber artist. My twin sister is also an artist; one of my brothers is a musician and hair stylist and my other brother a collector of wild and endangered animals. I grew up surrounded by art and the creative insanity that goes with it.

My parents were born in New York City, got married very young, as so many did in those days, moved to Dallas, Texas and had four children before they were in their mid-20s. Everything was creative. My father would paint and invent crazy (and not so crazy) things to sell; my mother would weave magical worlds in her wall hangings. She made everything, from our clothes to the ridiculously healthy meals (gray protein shakes with brewer's yeast and god-knows-what-else inside). She was a

Ingrid and her twin sister Sybil

ball of energy constantly doing something. Sometimes I would awake in the middle of the night to the noise of heavy objects being dragged across the floor. Rubbing my tired eyes in wonder, I would find my mom rearranging all the furniture in the house and polishing the wood floors. I thought this was normal. But I later learned that my home was far different from those of my friends.

Dallas in the late 1960s was a pretty conservative place. Bohemian families were

From left to right: Brothers, Peter and Jeffrey
Sister Ingrid and Sybil

certainly not the norm. My twin sister and I would be greeted at school dressed in our matching designer handmade outfits to wide-eyed wonder. My young and beautiful mother would come to PTA meetings dressed in her sexy modern clothes. She would raise more than a few eyebrows.

Mostly it was crazy and positive, but sometimes the stress of all those creative spirits in our home would turn dark. One day I witnessed my father burning all his paintings in a fit of rage and frustration. At the time, I thought, "If being an artist brings this kind of misery and pain, I don't want to be one." I vowed to live my life on the surface; never

to dig past the emotional barrier of my soul. Eventually, the creative pressure proved too much for my parents. They broke up when I was about 17 and divorced some time after that. From that point on, we all seemed to blow around, apart and together like leaves in a storm.

My sister and I started dancing and modeling professionally during our high school years. After graduating, we decided to go to Europe and try our luck there. We had quite a bit of success and a lot of adventure, perhaps more than 18 year-olds were ready for, but life decides what you can and can't handle. A little older and a lot wiser, we worked our way back to Dallas.

The next several years were spent doing various jobs. It was a dark time. My vow of living on the surface wasn't making me happy. I felt lost and rudderless.

Having a twin sister is a blessing. But it is hard to describe to those who don't have a twin. Sybil understands me in a way only a twin can understand the other. It's the same for me as well. We are unique parts of a greater whole: siblings, friends, confidants, and therapists, often feeling each other's joy and sorrow. So many times we will pick up the phone to tell each other of a certain event, only to learn the other had the same experience. I remember as a child, both of us being taken to the dentist for a check-up and finding the same cavity (our only one, ever) in the same place for both of us. It's not surprising we are both artists.

We challenge each other, of course, pointing out each other's flaws, competing to see who can do better. I prefer to see it as *inspiring* each other. We've taken turns leading each other through the forest of life. By the mid-1980s we had taken some interesting jobs (selling high-end computer systems, model-ing, acting), but I was still unsettled. A Swiss man, who had fallen in love with me while we were in Europe, came to Dallas to see me. He begged me to come back to Switzerland with him. He offered stability, consistency, and safety. The things I thought I needed. I said goodbye to Dallas and my family, not expect-ing to return.

In October of 1986, my middle brother, Pe-ter, had a terrible car accident, driving head-on into a concrete wall. He was thrown through the windshield and into the wall, breaking his neck. Peter is a great looking man. If he had

Ingrid and Sybil, Model Shoot

the temperament, he could have been a model. Calling Europe in those days was not like it is now. You did it for birthdays or emergen-cies. So when I heard my sister's voice on the phone, I knew it was bad news before she said hello. It grew worse from there. What would happen to Peter? Would he live, be disfig-ured, or ever walk again? We didn't know at the time. I spoke with my boyfriend and his

family. These dear people didn't hesitate to tell me that I must be with my family at this time. But it was my boyfriend who said with a kind of premonition, "If you leave now, you will never come back." I assured him that was nonsense, of course I would.

Peter was a body builder and health fanat-ic. Though he had a steel halo screwed into his skull to keep his neck straight, he never gave in to the dire predictions of the doctors. He was not disfigured nor was he destined to be an invalid. After coming home from the hospital, he moved into my apartment and I cared and watched over him as he healed. His recovery was nothing less than miracu-lous, far exceeding the doctor's expectations. Aside from tiny scars in his forehead where the stainless-steel screws went into his skull, there are no other lasting marks. We joked that it was his thick skull that saved him. I mused privately that maybe it was those hor-rible vitamin shakes my mom made us drink.

Several months had passed and Peter was now on his own, it was time to go back to Swit-zerland. But I couldn't. I now saw that it was not my path. It was not from lack of affection. It was just a nagging pull that it was the wrong direction, that something important was go-ing to happen; that Europe was not the place. If I went back there, I would probably lead a happy, ordinary life, but it was not my des-tiny and I knew it. I felt my inner voice call-ing, pulling me on. I followed my sister to Los Angeles to find what life had in store for me there. At least it would be different.

I have always felt and heard the quiet voice of what I like to call "my angel." It might be my higher self, intuition, an angel, even God. In the Talmud, it is said "every blade of grass has an angel over it whispering, *grow, grow.*" In Hinduism they call it Guru, or one's higher self, a greater spiritual mind that lives on a higher frequency or plane guiding our growth. Christianity talks about angels and our soul, metaphysics about spirit guides, and modern psychology simply calls it intuition, a leap of understanding from the subconscious mind. I leave it to each individual to discover his or her own belief and path. For me, this voice has been my guide, protecting me from danger and guiding me to my life's purpose. It is simple. When I listen, I always go the right way.

When I was a very young child, maybe three or four years old, my sister and I were outside playing in our front yard. It was a warm spring day in Texas, and my mother had left the screen door open so she could hear us. Two pretty blond twins by themselves playing in a suburban yard. We looked up and saw a black car drive past our house, slow down, then back up into our driveway. I remember it now, like watching a movie in my mind. There was a woman driving, too deep in the shadows to see, and a man sitting in the passenger seat. He opened his door and called to us. "Come on over, I have a special toy for you to play with. Come over, it's OK, your mom said you should get in and see the toy." My sister, Sybil, always the adventurous one, walked up to the open door to see this mysterious toy. I stood behind the open door looking into the man's face. I'll never forget his eyes. Cold and dead. He had a dark mole on his temple. My inner voice was now screaming "Evil. Stay away!" But at that age you are taught to listen to adults and trust their authority. I stood frozen in place. "Come in and you can have the toy," the woman urged. Sybil edged closer, barely a hand's grasp from this strange man, so curious about this special toy.

"Lunch time! Time to come in girls." My mother called from inside our home, oblivious to the dark drama unfolding in the driveway.

Sybil had been leaning into the open door, reaching for the toy. When she heard my mother's voice, she leaped back and said, "We have to eat lunch now. But you can join us." She brightened. "Come have lunch with us. I'll tell my mommy." They mumbled something, but didn't follow.

Once inside I told my mother about the strangers and the offer of a toy. Sybil asked if they could join us for lunch. My mother's eyes went wide and she bolted from the house. The car was facing outward for a quick escape and was already halfway down the block when we

Sybil on the left, Ingrid on the right
on their 5th birthday

reached the street. We saw it turn the corner and disappear. I still shudder to think how my life could have changed that day if my mother hadn't called when she did.

Once in Los Angeles, I found life not so different from Dallas. Jobs, nightlife, hangovers. The call for meaning scratched at my closed door. Once again it was a man who pulled me away, promising security and ease.

He was from New York City and was visiting Los Angeles. My sister wasn't pleased. "How can you be interested in this guy?" "I don't know," I said, "but I feel that he's going to take me to the place I'm supposed to be." Looking back, I realize how prophetic that was.

It all seems so quick, in retrospect. I was only in my mid-twenties. But at the time it seemed like a lifetime. I won't go into all the details, but give you just enough to know how I ended up in Aspen. We got married and I moved to New York City, where I was desperately unhappy, but put on a brave front. This was the man who was to lead me to my destiny, so why didn't it feel right? I made the most of my time in New York. One of my husband's acquaintances, a woman close to my mother's age, became a close friend. Her daughter had died of cancer as a teenager. My friend dedicated her life to finding a cure to childhood leukemia through cancer research and treatment. One of her goals was to raise enough money to add a special pediatric unit onto a prominent hospital in New York City. I helped with her fund raising efforts and am proud to have been a part of something so important. The pediatric cancer center, dedicated to her daughter's memory, was built in 2006 and helps many children to this day.

In the first summer of our marriage, my husband suggested we go to Aspen, Colorado for a vacation. I initially refused, not wanting to be around all the glitz and glamour I imagined there. He had family in Colorado, so he insisted. Of course, once there, I fell in love with the place, the mountains, the air. In my heart I felt I was finally home. After all these years of traveling and searching, I knew this was where I was supposed to be; where I would find my purpose. I cried most of the way on the flight back to New York. I had tasted my

destiny and saw where I was supposed to live.

In 1991 we moved to Snowmass Village (the ski town just outside of Aspen). I was only 26 years old, but it felt as if my life had been very long and complicated up to that point. I began to feel the thin air of the mountains

Aspen, Colorado

carrying me forward. I won't go into all the reasons I shouldn't have been married to my first husband. I will only say that it was a very poor fit. We were too different. He found my spiritual leanings foolish and had no interest in art or culture. I went out to find work so I would have some autonomy. That's when everything changed.

My friend (the one who built the cancer center) and her husband were visiting from New York. I told her that I wanted to work in an art gallery, to be around fine art. She was kind, but discouraged me heartily, "You have no experience, no art degree, not even a basic college degree, what can you offer?" She suggested I work at what I knew. I had done well selling high-end clothing in Los Angeles. There was plenty of that in Aspen. I know she was trying to be helpful but her words burned in me like a challenge rather than motherly advice. During my walks around Aspen, I enjoyed window-shopping. Every time I passed the Magidson Fine Art Gallery, I felt a strong pull.

Now things got interesting in my life, well, more interesting. It was a beautiful January afternoon, in 1992, clear and cold. The sky was cobalt blue, a color you see almost every day in the Rocky Mountains but never take for granted. I walked into the Magidson Fine Art Gallery to pick up an application, make an appointment or just see if there was a position available. Jay Magidson, the owner, was there in the back of the gallery. He stood up, walked up to me and said, "You've come for a job interview." It wasn't a question.

The previous salesperson had left in December. Jay had been running the gallery by himself since that time. He knew he needed help, but had hesitated to put an ad in the paper. "That's not how you get good employees," he mused. "The right one will come on his or her own."

David Begbie Opening at Magidson Fine Art, 2003

Jay and I sat down and talked about the job, art; a million things. I was supposed to take my friend and her husband to the airport that afternoon but stayed in the gallery, barely getting them there in time. We had talked for almost two hours. By the end of the interview, he offered me the job. Years later Jay told me

that he had fallen in love with me as soon as I walked in the door. He heard a voice in his head say, "That is the woman you should marry."

I started working as a salesperson for the Magidson Fine Art Gallery. It was a terrific job. The gallery was full of wonderful modern and contemporary masters and a handful of innovative emerging artists. Jay is a natural teacher and led me through whatever I didn't know, never embarrassing me. "Anyone can learn art history," he said, "but you are born knowing how to engage people, that's why I hired you." It didn't take long before I was selling art like a seasoned pro. I loved working there and getting away from my unpleasant home life.

Jay and I became great friends, sharing everything, sometimes talking an hour or two after closing. It was so easy, so natural. Don't get me wrong, it was never inappropriate. Jay knew I was married and never crossed that line. He had ended his own marriage years before and would never interfere in mine. Besides, I put on a great show of telling everyone how happily married I was. Jay had no reason to think there would ever be anything more than friendship. It was an odd time for me, split between these two worlds: on one side an unhappy marriage and on the other, art, friendship and a growing love for Jay. My heart was telling me that this was the man I was supposed to marry.

When I was very small I had a premonition. I knew I would marry and work with my best friend and we would have two children, a boy and a girl. It was such a simple and childish vision that I put it aside, though never forgetting it. During that first year of marriage, I would look sideways at my first husband and ask God, "You told me I would work with my

Eva Cellini, *Me*, oil on panel, 36 x 28 inches

nected with us in a profound and lasting way. I was drawn - no, that's not the right word - inspired by her work.

Eva was in her late 60s and I was in my late 20s when we met. The age difference meant nothing to us. We became great friends, sometimes speaking for hours on the phone. She probably won't admit this, but she is a philosopher and has taught me so much about life and art. During the years in the gallery, I sold dozens of her paintings, in love with each one. Sometimes I would regret seeing them go, but was always happy for the collector who got to own them. I have several of her works and am still inspired by them every day.

During the many times I visited Eva in New Jersey, I learned about the life of an artist. It was magical to me; intriguing and inspiring. I saw how she organized her home, her time and her life around her art. She did not paint at all hours of the night, wear ridiculous outfits or do any of the clichéd things that artists are reported to do. She was disciplined, focused and dedicated to her gift. Much later, when I was an artist myself, she told me, "An artist doesn't always have to be painting to be working. The process goes on all the time. You are thinking about it, dreaming about it, working out problems and challenges when you are going through your day, cooking, cleaning or

husband who would be my best friend. Why is it so difficult to work and be with this man? This can't be right."

About a year and half went by in this way and finally, my marriage was done. I called an attorney and moved into my own apartment. Shortly after that, Jay and I began dating, beginning a love affair that is 20 years old and counting.

Jay and I got married in June of 1996.

I continued to work with him at the gallery in Aspen, becoming his partner in every way. There are so many parts to running an art gallery, exciting and different from any other business. One unique aspect is working with the artists. Jay is naturally good at this. He says it is because he studied to be an artist as a youth. Maybe. But I think it takes something more, an honest curiosity and love for art. This was something we both deeply shared. One of the artists, Eva Cellini, con-

Eva Cellini and Ingrid

sleeping. You are always working." It was this advice that helped me realize that I had always been an artist, long before I picked up my first brush.

Eva is now 88 and still inspires me as an artist and as a person. Her age has slowed her down, but still she goes to her studio and paints nearly every day. Next to Jay, she is my best friend and mentor. I don't know if I would have made the leap to become an artist without her inspiration. I know it would have

Ingrid & Jay with Teagan & Isabella in their gallery

been much harder. I love you Eva.

Through the 1990s and into the early 2000s, Jay and I worked side by side in the gallery, making a wonderful life for ourselves. In 1998, we brought our first angel into the world, our daughter, Isabella. But I think I saw her long before that. Before I was pregnant, I woke to the vision of a young girl lying beside me in bed. She was turned away from me, her long dark hair lying on the pillow beside me. Her hair and chiffon blouse billowed

as if by a soft breeze. I felt so much peace and love. When I realized that I was awake and looking at an apparition, it disturbed the moment and the angel swirled away. Dream, vision, whatever you want to call it, I am convinced it was Isabella's spirit coming to me before she was born. She is a gift.

In October 2000, we had our second angel, a boy, Teagan. He is a ball of energy and wisdom, curious and alive. I am grateful for my children, how they have enriched my life and anchored me to this world. Any parent will share the challenges of raising children, but they will also share the immense love that they bring to your life.

Being an artist and mother is a unique challenge. There will always be bumps in the road, unexpected distractions and daily interruptions. However, I am reminded every day that I have been given a gift, that art and motherhood are my purpose and responsibility. And it is my obligation to give it back. But mostly I want to be an inspiration for my family.

While I didn't come to be an artist easily the creative force was always there. I resisted it terribly, unhappily going in different directions. It is easy to say that now, looking back. But looking forward in those years, I only saw unchanging sameness. It would take the anxiety of middle age to break through my carefully crafted walls.

Now I look forward, not at sameness, but at unending creativity and beauty. I wish this for every person alive - find what you love and do it.

One often meets his destiny on the road he takes to avoid it.

— JEAN DE LA FONTAINE

When you are inspired by some great purpose, some extraordinary project, all your thoughts break their bonds: Your mind transcends limitations, your consciousness expands in every direction, and you find yourself in a new, great and wonderful world. Dormant forces, faculties and talents become alive, and you discover yourself to be a greater person by far than you ever dreamed yourself to be.

— PATANJALI, AUTHOR OF
THE YOGA SUTRAS, CA. 150 B.C.

Madness of the Muses

AN INTRODUCTION BY JAY MAGIDSON

*I*NSPIRATION often shows up in strange ways and when least expected.

It is not surprising Ingrid became an artist. Her parents are artists after all. The former New Yorkers, living in Dallas, Texas would drag their four reluctant children to museums and galleries on the weekends, determined to expose them to culture. It would be many years, however, before the seeds would take root.

In late 2005, approaching forty, Ingrid felt an uncomfortable pressure that would cause an upheaval and change that would ripple forward in her life and around those close to her. The feeling began as a sense of something missing, a discomfort, an itch. By this time, Ingrid had been working with me in our art gallery in Aspen, Colorado for nearly fifteen years. Surrounded by art and artists, she suddenly craved more, much more.

One evening, unable to contain the pressure to create any longer, she blurted out: "I need space."

The worst thoughts came to my mind, but I asked her to tell me what she meant.

Isabella in Ingrid's first Studio, 2006

Love will Return, 2006 - In collaboration with Eva Cellini, this was Ingrid's first exhibited and sold work

"I need a place to create. You have an office. Our kids have their rooms. I need my own space too."

There was a third bay in the garage of our home that was being used for art storage. I asked if I cleaned that out, would it work for her. Ingrid simply nodded, not even sure what she had in mind or what she was going to do in her "studio."

This new studio, ironically, had some of the best views of our home. Yet with the roll door closed, the tiny four windows were too high to show any of it. It was very small, about 10 by 14 feet, dark and raw. It looked like what it was - an empty garage.

But this poorly lit space with its concrete floor and plywood walls, this new studio was now hers, to use as she pleased. But for what? Neither of us knew. Ingrid was grateful to have a place to create, to express the ideas burning to get out.

The next several months were extremely difficult. Ingrid would spend her evenings in her new studio brooding about being an artist, experimenting with the thousands of ideas spinning in her head. She had no formal art training, no experience and no instructors. Doubt threatened to derail everything. But the quiet voice had grown louder, more demanding each night. So she pressed on.

Ingrid thought of all the paintings she had seen in the museums in her youth. "How many paintings are sitting in basements and storage areas, rarely seen?" It was as if the people in those portraits were calling to her across time. A piece of their spirit was captured on canvas then trapped in the dark recesses of museum storage. Wasn't her studio a converted storage room and therefore a link to their mutual captivity? They were bound to portraiture; she was driven to express it and release them. Ingrid felt a vaporous cord of connection grow, leading her to her destiny.

"I want them to breathe, to live again. I want them to be here and in their own time simultaneously. My art will be transparent, ghostlike, so the viewer can see both worlds," she announced.

"How will you do that?" I asked.

Secret Passions - an early piece that was later abandoned

"I don't know." She said.

Ingrid nervously took up smoking cigarettes and drinking late into the nights and early mornings. This was perhaps the darkest

Soar Away with Me, 2006
An early piece that was later abandoned

Ingrid was digging into her soul for inspiration and guidance, a painful process many artists understand. It is a lonely road. Others might offer advice, but ultimately there are no partners in art. Artist Eva Cellini describes it as a kind of "Sweet Torture;" another artist says simply, "The mind travels alone." Call it inspiration, an inner voice, creativity, but truly it is the song of the muses, the indescribable creative force that exists around us. These inspirational creatures have only one rule. The recipient of their aid must ask for their help.

By mid-2006 Ingrid's works began to show final form. There was still much to accomplish, but she had made a breakthrough. Ingrid put a few of her works in the Aspen gallery to see what would happen. One small piece, a collaboration with Eva Cellini's work, sold in a few days. The others languished on the walls without comment or attention.

Although disappointed, Ingrid never stopped working, pushing past more technical

time for us and our family. Every artist knows the dim void that threatens to consume them. The pull from both sides, from the normal and mundane, predictable, "safe" world, to the creative force that demands the impossible - to create what has never been made before. Art is a supreme act of hubris, after all, as if calling to the world, "I will be the one who brings the unknown forward."

Ingrid's perseverance paid off. Her works began to show form and the earliest experimental works began to appear. It was immediately clear she was on to something unique and exciting. But the challenges were monumental, half technical; half artistic, all looming large before her. These early creations touched on her idea to make an image float, a ghost of its ancient self. The concept was there, but they were still only experiments, raw and unrefined. It would be some time before presentable work would be ready. Ingrid pressed on, the greatest testament to her belief in her idea and her muses.

Just a Shadow Now, 2006
An early piece that was later abandoned

obstacles, creating greater dimension in the work. In late 2006 she made another technical and artistic breakthrough, which continues to define her work. She left space between the layers.

The results were breathtaking. In my excitement, I suggested a one woman show in July of 2007 at our Aspen gallery. At this point, only two of Ingrid's works had sold, neither of them used the new technique. No one had seen the new work or given feedback on its collectability. It was a risky gamble artistically and financially. July is one of the busiest months of the year in Aspen and galleries always put up their best-selling artists during this time. If the show failed, it would weigh heavily on both the gallery and Ingrid's artistic ego. The date was set for its numerical uniqueness: July 7, 2007 or 7-7-7.

I pulled all of Ingrid's older pieces from the gallery. The plan was to make a splash, reveal the new work at the show and not before. In

Mr. & Mrs. Siwak with Ingrid and *Surrealism Lives in Me,* the work they purchased at Ingrid's First exhibition

Brad & Penny Place with Ingrid and *Temptation,* the first piece purchased at Ingrid's First exhibition

preparation for the exhibition, Ingrid buried herself in her tiny studio, simultaneously excited and terrified at the prospect before her. She had helped organize dozens of art exhibitions at the gallery. Many went well; some didn't sell a thing. She knew what was pos-

sible and fought off the fears and doubts that crush so many talented artists. The voices of the muses pushed her on.

The exhibition was planned. It would consist of twelve works, most of them large, one over six feet tall. All would be framed and consist of multiple layers of acrylic, antique objects, collage and her now trademark butterflies. Ingrid would have to accomplish all this in less than six months in her 10 x 14 foot studio. It was a monumental challenge both physically and artistically.

Life goes on despite our lofty goals and plans. Ingrid was still a mother of two small children whose needs she refused to ignore. Ingrid worked long into the nights, emerging from the studio as the sun rose, exhausted and spent, sometimes exhilarated by the results, other times disappointed and disgusted. But she never quit.

Early June arrived. The children were out of school, there was a household to run, the demands of a small business and the completion of an entire exhibition. The show invitation sailed out to the gallery's mailing list, over 4,000 past and prospective clients. How would they react? Would they ignore this show as an obvious act of nepotism or come to the opening reception to embrace a new artist? Ingrid and I would soon find out.

The first inquiry came from Brad Place.

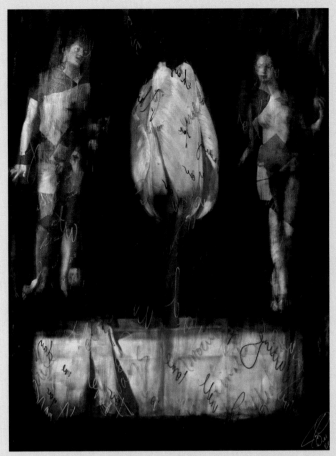

From the Beginning to the End of Time, 2006
An early piece that was later abandoned

Brad and Penny Place are avid art collectors but had never bought anything from the Magidson Fine Art Gallery in Aspen. They had stepped in a few times to look at the art, but had never found anything they liked enough to buy. Brad's call in mid-June would be the first of many involving Ingrid's work as well as the beginning of a very close friendship.

He asked what pieces were available and could he see them before the opening reception. Brad explained that he would be unable to make the opening but wanted to see the work with the goal of acquiring one. It was arranged that Brad would come to Aspen a few weeks early and see a preview of the show. Most of the pieces were still being framed; only a handful was available to view.

Brad barely hid his excitement. Ingrid's work was among the most interesting art he had seen in years, and he wasn't going to let it

slip away. He asked Ingrid which was her favorite piece. She told him about "Temptation," a large vertical piece of Eve in the Garden of Eden. In the work, Eve is presented seductively holding an apple, wrapped in musical notes and handmade paper. The piece, unfinished and unframed, could only be shown to Brad in a small digital photograph. He bought it on the spot. The gates had opened.

It takes time to hang an exhibition. Even a small exhibition takes a full day. Larger shows like Ingrid's can take two or more days, first to take down the existing art, then to arrange, hang and light the new works. Labels, price lists, photographs, website updates and a hundred other things must be done. Ingrid's new works were brought into the gallery on the Tuesday before the Saturday opening to allow plenty of time for the installation. Some galleries will lock the doors during installation so they can focus on the tasks at hand. However, as Wednesday was the Fourth of July, a very busy day in Aspen, closing the gallery was not an option. The installation would just have to be done during business hours.

Twelve works by the unknown new artist, Ingrid Dee Magidson, were lovingly placed in the empty gallery for installation on the Tuesday before the Saturday opening. By Wednesday afternoon the entire exhibition was sold out. Not a single piece of Ingrid's art made it onto the wall before being purchased.

The opening reception was held on Saturday, 7-7-7, to an overflowing crowd. Butterflies were released into the room in celebration while friends and collectors admired the unusual new work of Ingrid Dee Magidson. There were plenty of questions, but the most common one, "I didn't know you were an artist, where did this come from?" was answered with the only response possible, "from the muses."

Ingrid's career was launched.

TEMPTATION, 2007

Temptation

AN INTRODUCTION BY BRADLEY E. PLACE, JR.

S a lover of history, I have always been fascinated with art from the Renaissance and Baroque periods, even before I knew those periods had names. The paintings of Leonardo da Vinci, Michelangelo, Raphael, Titian, Rubens and Caravaggio are regarded as some of the finest in history. Their enigmatic portraits of kings and queens, nobility, courtiers and long gone religious leaders depict their subjects as they would be remembered for eternity. The paintings almost succeed in bringing their subjects back to life, memorializing them in time. I always wondered, who were those people and what do their portraits tell us about their lives? Were they really who

they appear to be? Or were these works fictional versions of who they wanted us to believe them to be?

Late in the afternoon of a particularly hot day in June, 2007, I walked to the mail box and pulled out a handful of bills and junk mail. As I shuffled through the pile, a mailer from the Magidson Fine Art Gallery, Aspen, Colorado fell to the ground. When I picked it up I saw a style of art I had never seen before. I was immediately captivated. It was an image of what appeared to be a "contemporized" Renaissance figure that was clearly from the period, yet was very different from any Renaissance art I had ever encountered before.

It looked classical in every sense, yet there was something else going on, something ethereal that transformed the portrait from an historical "snapshot" in time into something new and demanding of further exploration. For me the 500 year-old portrait on the brochure I was holding had come alive! It was so arresting that I called the gallery and made an appointment to meet the artist early the

Invitation for Ingrid's first exhibition at Magidson Fine Art, Aspen

INGRID DEE MAGIDSON
JULY 7 – JULY 21, 2007

PAST BECOMES PRESENT

OPENING RECEPTION FOR THE ARTIST
SATURDAY, JULY 7, 6 – 8

A PORTION OF THE PROCEEDS OF THIS EXHIBITION WILL BE DONATED TO THE VOICES OF TOMORROW FOUNDATION, A NOT FOR PROFIT CORPORATION HELPING CHILDREN AND THE ARTS IN THE ROARING FORK VALLEY.

PAST BECOMES PRESENT

next day to see this new art form for myself. I drove to Aspen early the next morning and arrived at the gallery twenty minutes before it was scheduled to open. I could see the artist, Ingrid Magidson, through the front window, busily assembling the unframed work that would become one of the first examples of what we now consider to be her distinctive style.

The propped up, unfinished work was not only amazing in its construction; it was also captivating in its appearance. My immediate reaction was to buy the work right on the spot. But I then thought to ask Ingrid if she was working on any other pieces that she might favor more? She replied that her personal favorite just happened to be a particular piece she was working on back in her studio. I immediately said, "Well, then, that's the one I'd like to buy!" She informed me the name of the piece was "Temptation" and that it was still a

few days away from being completed. I happily paid for "Temptation", right there, sight unseen, and left the gallery feeling both elated to have encountered this new, transformative style of art, but also a bit disappointed to have nothing other than an invoice marked "paid" to take home with me.

What I know now but didn't know then is that Ingrid's favorite work is always the piece she is currently working on. Over the years, my wife Penny and I, have continued to collect her works, all of which were once her favorites. Now they're our favorites. If you bait a trap with Ingrid's "favorite work", it seems you will catch us every time! We have collected a number of her works, including a large commission currently being created. The commission will merge Goya's two famous portraits of the Duchess of Alba (the "Black Duchess" and the "White Duchess") into a single, dramatic work. Upon completion it will stand nearly eight feet tall. We also have several smaller pieces in our collection that are absolutely riveting. One of them, entitled "The Queen of Hearts", is a particular favorite of ours and hangs over the fireplace in our bedroom. I often look at it and wonder how Ingrid worked her magic and created it; and what the "Queen of Hearts" means to her and what it means to me.

The rest, as they say, is history. Not only was "Temptation" a powerful work depicting the very first woman, Eve, holding the apple in the Garden of Eden, it was the first of Ingrid's work in her signature style and the first piece of hers that we collected. Although her work continues to develop and evolve, her early works were completed using many of the same fundamental techniques she uses in her process today. Ingrid continues to experiment and innovate with new ideas, materials and techniques to form and enhance her ethereal images and further test the boundaries of her art form as well as her own creativity.

Queen of Hearts, 2012

Today, approximately 175 pieces of Ingrid's creations live on the walls of collectors and art buyers throughout the world. Their owners are as diverse and interesting as the Ingrid's subject matter. Her creations have grown in complexity from using three layers in "Temptation," to as many as six, as well as embedding treasures and objects within that are often only discovered over time and through many observations.

Ingrid's focus and dedication to her art provides her with ever expanding opportunities to explore and redefine her artistic journey as she travels through the fascinating and historic hallways of the Renaissance and Baroque eras.

Ingrid Magidson, *Past Becomes Present*: July 7 to July 21, 2007

by Stewart Oksenhorn, Arts Editor

ASPEN - In her teen years and her 20s, Ingrid Magidson discovered a taste for sales. She worked first for a computer firm in her native Texas, and then for a series of high-end shops on Rodeo Drive. What attracted her was the stuff that most people find dull about selling: following up with customers, building relationships with clients. When she took a job at Magidson Fine Art some 15 years ago - and then married the boss, Jay Magidson, and became a co-owner of the Aspen gallery - she specialized in selling, leaving the seemingly more dynamic task of handling artists to her husband. Ingrid finds more satisfaction in selling than in the "glamour" job she had as a teenager - modeling, in Dallas and then Europe, usually in tandem with her twin sister, Sybil.

It wasn't exactly an artist's temperament, then, that lived in Magidson. When she said, in an interview with The Aspen Times - "They eat, drink and sleep it. They'll sacrifice anything, even their families, for their art. That's the passion Jay and I love." - she was speaking about the artists that show at the gallery. She most definitely was not referring to herself.

But that statement was made a little more than two years ago, just as Magidson was staring at the final days of being in her 30s. A few weeks later, she had turned into a different sort of being.

"When I turned 40, something snapped in me," said Magidson. "I withdrew into myself, and I didn't know why. I didn't feel like I was living my life. I started to dig deep inside and wrote poetry, really profound poetry.

"If you asked me, at 39, if I would be going crazy like this, I'd say, 'Yeah, right.' But I fell into it hard."

That fall into the creative realm has meant many nights in a tiny studio, where she has traded sleep for the pursuit of her art. It has meant tuning into the voices she hears in her head; it has meant anguish and frustration.

And it has translated into a body of work, the first Magidson is ever showing publicly. Her art - which combines her poetry, Renaissance-era images, butterflies and a computer-driven, three-dimensional technique that she declines to reveal in any detail - is featured in a show at Magidson Fine Art which opens with a reception Saturday from 6-8 p.m.

Ingrid Magidson - then Ingrid Hill - was surrounded by art as a child. Her father, Irving, is an inventor and artist, who now lives near Redstone. Her mother, Elaine, is an artist. Ingrid herself messed around with her father's materials, making 3-D boxed sculptures out of scraps of frame. She mostly abandoned actually making anything, but the creative process seems to have continued between her ears.

"She's been thinking of these ideas for years," said Jay Magidson, whose own creative desires are expressed in running the gallery, and in writing sci-fi. "And then they came into a culmination, to a focal point, and it breaks out into the physical world. That happened

a year ago, when the technical stuff worked out and she just took off."

In her inner vision, Ingrid had ideas of what she wanted: transparent images, illumination, music, butterflies, images seen through other images. Translating that so others could see it was an often agonizing process.

"I was smoking and drinking and just going crazy," said Ingrid, the mother of two kids, 9 and 6. "Those were very hard times for me. It was trial and error, sitting in my studio all night, lots of nights, frustrated, trying to figure it all out. Thank god I had friends I could call at 4 in the morning."

And there were the sorts of friends who you can't get on the phone at any hour. Magidson's collages are inspired by beings she likens to angels: Joan of Arc, the surrealists Salvador Dalí and Rene Magritte, Puccini. (Other inspirations are those who do pick up the phone: Ingrid's husband and parents; Eva Cellini, an 82-year-old artist who shows at Magidson Fine Art.)

"I love people who do great things in life. I've met people who have such a profound impact on me, and I take what I feel, what I read," said Magidson, who is presenting her work under the name Ingrid Dee (Dee is her middle name). "I take their energy, what they do for me, how they lift me, and put it in the work."

The first piece from the current exhibit that she completed was "Voices in My Head," something of a self-reflection. The piece is relatively uncomplicated, but in the scribblings of verse in the work is conveyed the energy Magidson brings to the art, and even the breakthrough that the piece represents. "This was an intense night. This was the discovery of all this," she said. "It was me going crazy."

The technical breakthrough was a relief, but also a challenge. "This fear set in. This fear - did I want to keep going there? Did I want to spend all the money on materials?" Magidson said. She did continue, and a sense of peacefulness came into the art. Where "Voices in My Head" contains an unbridled

energy, successive works became more about a complex, considered ideal of beauty. The pieces - "Queen of the House," dedicated to her mother; "La bohème," for her husband, an opera enthusiast; "Surrealism Lives in Me," for Dalí and Magritte - combine sheet music with found objects and borrowed portraits by Renaissance giants da Vinci, Correggio and Titian in a captivating layered effect. Magidson prefers to address the emotional impact rather than the process.

"Art today is so literal and angry and about war and hate," said Magidson, who credits Jay for helping her work out the computer side of the technique. "I understand artists are trying to express themselves. But I want the beauty of the Renaissance period. I wanted to bring that back. I want people to feel beauty - or sadness, some kind of intensity."

Bringing other worlds - the past, the hidden - into this world is a big part of Magidson's motivation. "I become a voice for these souls," she said, referring to the Renaissance painters whose images she uses, and the figures who have inspired her work. "A lot of these paintings, these people, nobody gets to see them anymore. They're tucked away in storage, in museums, and I want people to see them in a new way. "People should ask these profound questions: Are there soulmates? What happens after we die?"

More or less hidden in the art are the butterflies. But each work has a butterfly image; in "Alive in Me," the butterfly appears as a mask. At tomorrow's opening reception, Magidson plans to release a swarm of butterflies. (There will also be a string quartet from the

Aspen Music School performing.) Magidson talks about the butterfly as a symbol: "Butterflies are something that are here so briefly, so delicate and fragile and beautiful. That's sort of my signature."

But she doesn't specifically relate the butterfly to herself. She doesn't point out the connection between the butterfly and her own mental fragility that has had her despairing over her life's purpose, spending sleepless nights in an eight-by-12 foot studio that barely fits her art.

Maybe that's because she isn't so fragile and short-lived. Magidson considers her dark period at an end. There are still nights spent awake, but there is a different quality to them.

"I thought, 'OK, I've figured it out, now I'll be OK,'" she said, referring to overcoming the technical hurdles a few months ago. "No. Now I'm driven to produce the work. I don't sleep anymore. Because I can't stop working.

"But the frustration is gone. I'm at peace, understanding where I'm going with it."

Stewart Oksenhorn's e-mail address is stewart@aspentimes.com

The article above from *The Aspen Times,* July 7, 2007 is reprinted here in its entirety with the permission of its author.

2007

Desire's Web

Tangled threads of Life
Thrust into my hands
It calls
"Untangle me, undo life's knotted maze!"

But pushed aside to weave the methodical calling
Comforted as wife, woman, parent, provider.

I cannot resist, temptation takes me. Slowly, I reach
Grasping the tangled mass, separating the fibers and threads:
Pain, pleasure, frustration, inspiration, fear…madness.

Tirelessly reweaving these into my work
Finally creating a web of sense for my existence.

— Ingrid Dee Magidson, 2007

Voices in My Head, 2007

It took six thousand years to produce her; her like will not be seen in the earth again in fifty thousand.

- MARK TWAIN

Why should the artist be troubled by the shrill clamor of criticism? Why should those who cannot create take upon themselves to estimate the value of creative work? What can they know about it? If a man's work is easy to understand, an explanation is unnecessary…And if his work is incomprehensible, an explanation is wicked.

— OSCAR WILDE

HOMAGE TO EVA, 2007

A true artist is not one who is inspired, but one who inspires others.

- SALVADOR DALÍ

DALÍESQUE, 2007

QUEEN OF THE HOUSE, 2007

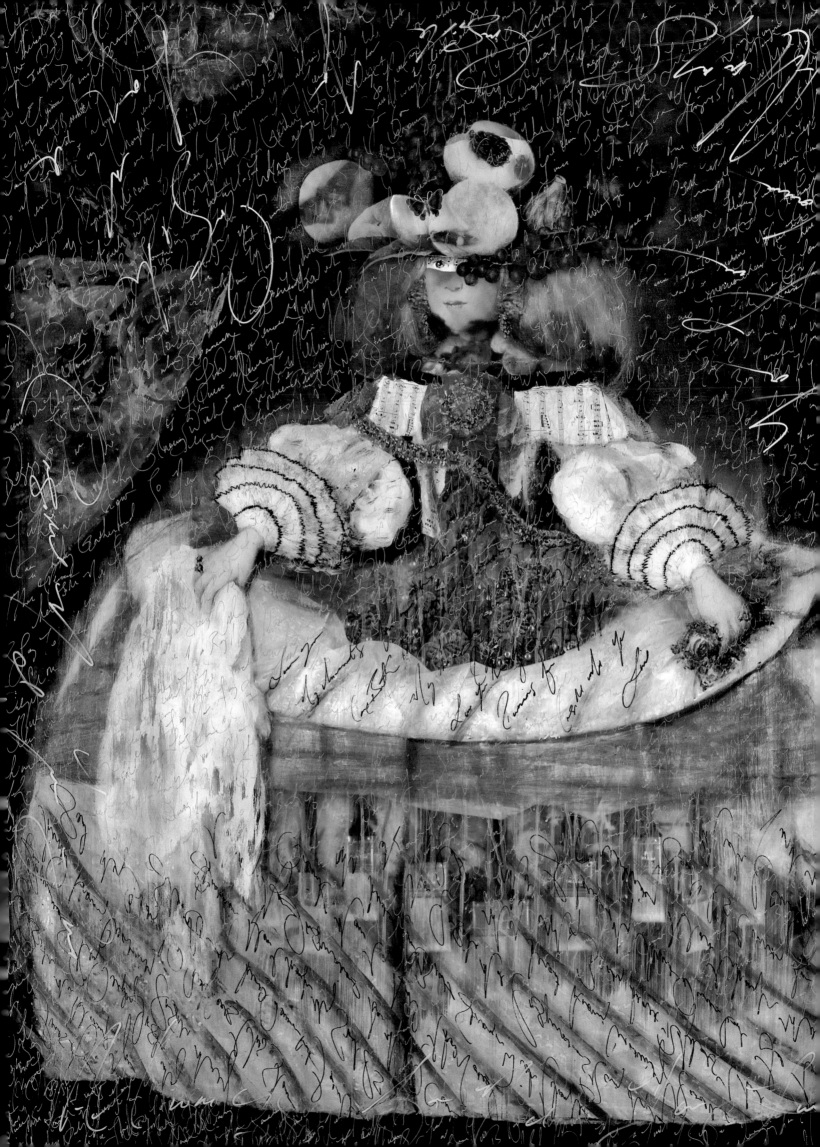

2008

*The meaning of life is to
find your gift,
the purpose of life is to
give it away.*

— Pablo Picasso

THE TEMPTRESS, 2008

Painting is poetry that is seen rather than felt, and poetry is painting that is felt rather than seen.

— Leonardo da Vinci

Always Connected, 2008

The King has Landed, 2008

BIRTH OF A WOMAN, 2008

45

BUDHALISQUE, 2008

PRINCESS BLUE, 2008

Drink Deeply at My Eyes

Through the smoke of time
Looking to the forgotten now,
At loves and lives lost
All adding up to a timeless face
A beautiful face with piercing eyes

Then nature pulled aside her verdant veil
For me, another chance, a moment brief,
To glimpse my children's children...
Before me.

Ah, drink deeply at my eyes
My hazy vision of the future,
Written eons ago,
Before there was a word for time
When the very fabric of life
Was but a glimmer of spirit
When God breathed a sign,
And I was born.

— Jay Magidson

Timeless Beauty, 2008

*D*estiny is no matter of chance. It is a matter of choice. It is not a thing to be waited for, it is a thing to be achieved.

— WILLIAM JENNINGS BRYAN

In Silence They Speak, 2008

Heirloom, 2008

53

Fairytales, 2008

2009

Who Will Know Your Heart?

The path you choose
is different from the rest
Full of rocks and cliffs and thorns
But richer is the view.

Oh brief taper flickering in the wind
So fragile is your flame
But stronger is your glow

'tis but a moment on this mortal stage
Endless fields and oceans abound
All gone in a blink

Ah, to linger but a second more,
To lie beside your love
Surely there's time for that.

For when the fuel's spent,
And the flame can burn no more
Who will know your heart?

— JAY MAGIDSON

*G*ood morning, on July 7

Though still in bed, my thoughts go out to you, my Immortal

Beloved, now and then joyfully, then sadly, waiting to learn

whether or not fate will hear us - I can live only wholly

with you or not at all - Yes, I am resolved to wander so long away from you

until I can fly to your arms and say that I am really at home with you, and

can send my soul enwrapped in you into the land of spirits - Yes, unhappily

it must be so - You will be the more contained since you know my fidelity

to you. No one else can ever possess my heart - never - never - Oh God,

why must one be parted from one whom one so loves. And yet my life in V

is now a wretched life - Your love makes me at once the happiest and the

unhappiest of men - At my age I need a steady, quiet life - can that be so

in our connection? My angel, I have just been told that the mailcoach goes

every day - therefore I must close at once so that you may receive the letter

at once - Be calm, only by a calm consideration of our existence can we

achieve our purpose to live together - Be calm - love me - today - yesterday -

what tearful longings for you - you - you - my life - my all - farewell. Oh

continue to love me - never misjudge the most faithful heart of your beloved.

Ever thine, ever mine, ever ours

— LUDWIG VON BEETHOVEN, LETTER TO HIS UNKNOWN BELOVED, CA. 1812

BEETHOVEN'S MUSE, 2009

Mortal Desires, 2009

ALWAYS AND FOREVER, 2009

Seductress

You lie liquid on your throne
Sublime beauty, your thoughts a mystery

In bosom's chest you hide
A lover lost, so many years,
So many thoughts ago.

But our minds wander
And go empty at a glance
For it is you we desire

ASPEN MEMORIES, 2009

And with that look,
We melt with passion,
Your heart ignored,
So lost in our own.

We fall into your eyes
And toss our souls to the ground
Soft cushions
For your perfect feet.

— JAY MAGIDSON

I feel there is nothing more truly artistic than to love.

— Vincent Van Gogh

Princess Ariel, 2009

Dissi d'arte, vissi d'amore

"I LIVED FOR ART, I LIVED FOR LOVE."
— PUCCINI, *TOSCA*, 1895

ESSENCE OF WOMAN, 2009

2010

Life's Echo

Formless souls slide by
Life's echo, they wander
Past my eyes.

Their light so faint,
They choose the night
To shine their warning flame.

And I listen to their whispers
Memories like sighs
Dreams, suspired hopes

They're drawn to my art
My painted stories
Mixed by time and pain

We share the evening's dance
Distant friends and lovers
Touched, but not...touched.

— Jay Magidson

God explained many things...but he never explained...this cryptic statement...He causes things to look different so it would appear time has passed.

— Philip K. Dick, *VALIS* 1981

My work is about change, metamorphosis, how one life transforms from physical to spiritual or spiritual to physical. Each subject I choose for my work is alive to me, not in a metaphorical sense, but truly alive. They have personality, memories, desires, loves; everything you and I have. Only they are frozen in time. I listen to them carefully, "what do you want?" And they guide me - to put a butterfly, a watch, a feather, an ancient picture or some other forgotten object into the work. It is their world. The most important thing I can do as an artist is listen. When they are in my studio, we are each other's guests. They will be traveling soon. I leave the music on at night so they don't get lonely while they are here. I'm never sorry to see them go, to live on in this new form. I know there'll be others.

— INGRID DEE MAGIDSON

Metamorphosis, 2010

Positively Primitive, 2010

LIFE'S TREASURES, 2010

It is not the critic who counts; not the man who points out how the strong man stumbles...the credit belongs to the man in the arena, whose face is marred by dust and sweat and blood; who strives valiantly; who at his worst, if he fails, at least fails while daring greatly, so that his place shall never be with those cold and timid souls who neither know victory nor defeat.

— THEODORE "TEDDY" ROOSEVELT,
1910 SPEECH AT THE SORBONNE, PARIS

STRENGTH AND HONOR, 2010

*In our life there is a
single color,
as on an artist's palette,
which provides the
meaning of life and art.
It is the color of love.*

— Marc Chagall

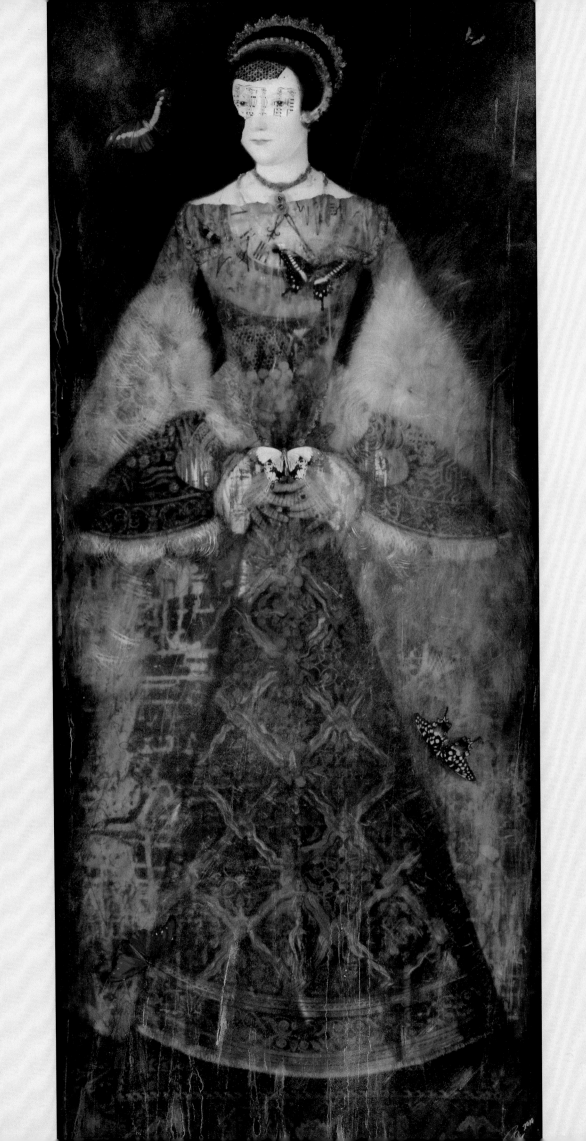

Not just beautiful,
though – the stars
are like the trees in
the forest, alive and
breathing. And they're watching
me.

— HARUKI MURAKAMI, *KAFKA ON THE SHORE*

NIGHT'S MELODY, 2010

Beauty is eternity gazing at itself in a mirror.

— KAHLIL GIBRAN

The Road Not Taken

Two roads diverged in a yellow wood,
And sorry I could not travel both
And be one traveler, long I stood
And looked down one as far as I could
To where it bent in the undergrowth;

Then took the other, as just as fair,
And having perhaps the better claim,
Because it was grassy and wanted wear;
Though as for that the passing there
Had worn them really about the same,

And both that morning equally lay
In leaves no step had trodden black.
Oh, I kept the first for another day!
Yet knowing how way leads on to way,
I doubted if I should ever come back.

I shall be telling this with a sigh
Somewhere ages and ages hence:
Two roads diverged in a wood, and I—
I took the one less traveled by,
And that has made all the difference.

— ROBERT FROST, 1916

THE ROAD LESS TRAVELED, 2010

To send light into the darkness of men's hearts - such is the duty of the artist.

— ROBERT SCHUMANN

2011

To be creative means to be in love with life. You can be creative only if you love life enough that you want to enhance its beauty, you want to bring a little more music to it, a little more poetry to it, a little more dance to it."

— OSHO

ILLUMINATION, 2011

When one tugs at a single thing in nature, he finds it attached to the rest of the world.

— John Muir

I sleep, but my heart waketh. It is the voice of my beloved that knocketh, saying, Open to me, my love, my dove, my undefiled. For my head is filled with dew, and my locks with the drops of the night.

— SONG OF SOLOMON

YOUR WORDS AWAKEN MY SLEEPING HEART, 2011

I want to see you.
Know your voice.

Recognize you when you
first come 'round the corner.

Sense your scent when I come
into a room you've just left.

Know the lift of your heel,
the glide of your foot.

Become familiar with the way
you purse your lips
then let them part,
just the slightest bit,
when I lean in to your space
and kiss you.

I want to know the joy
of how you whisper
"more"

— RŪMĪ, *I WANT TO SEE YOU*, CA. 1260

A MOMENT IN TIME, 2011
PREVIOUS PAGE: ALWAYS DEAR TO MY HEART, 2011

I almost wish we were
        butterflies and liv'd but
        three summer days – three
        such days with you I could
fill with more delight than fifty common
        years could ever contain.

— JOHN KEATS

PROFOUNDLY YOURS, 2011

PEACEFUL JOURNEY BROTHER, 2011

2012

Music is a moral law. It gives a soul to the universe, wings to the mind, flight to the imagination, a charm to sadness, and life to everything. It is the essence of order, and leads to all that is good, just and beautiful, of which it is the invisible, but nevertheless dazzling, passionate, and eternal form.

— PLATO

QUEEN OF HEARTS, 2012

Words Social Forum

CENTRO SOCIALE DELL'ARTE

INGRID DEE MAGIDSON – INCARNAZIONI

Ingrid Dee Magidson is an American artist born in Dallas, Texas. She lives and works in Aspen, Colorado, where she's got her studio and creates her beautiful work. Ingrid's work is in notable collections throughout the world, including: Antonio Banderas & Melanie Griffith, NYC; Jackie Bezos, Seattle; Sarah & Gideon Gartner, NYC; and Sam & Cheryl Wyly, Aspen/Dallas. Inventor of a spectacular layering technique on which her work is based, Ingrid allows a journey through the time opening an ideal window on past times, offering a passage of interchange between the character and the viewer. Her creative vein is strongly pervaded by an unlimited faith in the artist's sensibility through which her characters talk and tell about their worlds and emotions. Her starting idea is to believe in the subjects she depicts, in their lives and deeds; doing this the artist creates a continuum space time connection the viewer can cross to enter the heart of the work. Her

Ingrid Dee Magidson è un'artista statunitense originaria di Dallas, Texas. Vive e lavora ad Aspen, Colorado, dove ha il suo studio e crea le sue stupefacenti opere d'Arte. Famosa in tutto il mondo, le sue opere fanno parte di notevoli collezioni fra cui: Antonio Banderas & Melanie Griffith, NYC; Jackie Bezos, Seattle; Sarah & Gideon Gartner, NYC; and Sam & Cheryl Wyly, Aspen/Dallas. Ideatrice di una spettacolare tecnica "a strati" su cui si basa il suo lavoro, Ingrid rende possibile un viaggio attraverso il Tempo, aprendo una finestra ideale su epoche passate, offrendo un passaggio di interscambio fra i personaggi protagonisti e lo spettatore che ammira le sue opere. La sua vena creativa è tenacemente percorsa da una fede illimitata nella sensibilità soggettiva dell'artista, tramite attraverso cui i suoi personaggi parlano e raccontano i loro mondi e le loro emozioni. La sua idea di partenza è quella di credere fortemente nei soggetti che

hand is just a mere means which allows the Art to give us back the Beauty and the Truth of the depicted characters, it's a jump toward the re-creation of a vanished past that's still present, talking and has a life of its own. Her magic takes the breath away and makes jump. Every time you observe an Ingrid's piece of work, life (re)appears and comes into the world again, it comes back to us like a dream first, then like an inescapable pictorial matter, material, scanning the whole expanded senses that become six. The sixth sense is the last stage you come to when observing a Magidson's piece of Art. If you are able to cross it, it is possible you go into a trance. Hypnotic, delicate, haunting, enigmatic, deep, the subjects of Ingrid look at us holding out one hand, finally talking us about their new incarnation. I interviewed this extraordinary artist for WSF. Enjoy.

FG: Welcome on WSF, Ingrid. Thank you for being here. When did you start your artistic career and how would you define your Art?

IM: *My career developed in two stages. Both my parents are artists and often took me to museums as a child. Once they told me there are far more pieces in the basement than on the walls. That got me thinking, was there a way to bring these painting into the light so more people could see them. This thought never left me. I went through many other careers until I began working for an art gallery in Aspen. The owner is now my husband of 16 years. Being in a gallery exposed me to a lot of art and artists. My original idea continued to stir in my subconscious until 2005 when it burst to the surface. In a flurry of experimentation I came up with my current technique of layering renaissance images on transparent*

ritrae, nelle loro vite, nelle loro imprese; in questo modo l'artista getta un ponte spazio temporale che lo spettatore finale potrà varcare per inoltrarsi nel vero cuore dell'opera. La sua mano è solo un mezzo che permette all'Arte di restituire a noi la Bellezza e la Verità dei protagonisti ritratti, è un salto verso la ri-creazione di un passato svanito eppure ancora presente e parlante, vivente, pregno di vita propria. Una magia che lascia senza fiato e fa rabbrividire d'emozione. Ogni volta che si osserva un quadro di Ingrid, ecco che la vita (ri)appare e (ri)viene al mondo, ritorna a noi prima come un sogno, poi come un'ineludibile materia pittorica, materica, scansionando tutti i sensi, che si estendono e diventano sei. Il sesto senso è l'ultimo stadio a cui si approda dall'osservazione di un quadro della Magidson e se si riesce ad oltrepassarlo è possibile, molto probabile, che ci si addormenti in un trance profondo. Ipnotici, delicati, ammalianti, enigmatici, profondi, i personaggi della Magidson ci guardano tendendoci una mano, e infine ci parlano dalla loro nuova incarnazione. Ho intervistato questa straordinaria artista per WSF. Enjoy.

FG. Benvenuta su WSF, Ingrid. Grazie di essere qui. Quando hai iniziato la tua carriera artistica e come definiresti la tua Arte?

I. *La mia carriera si è sviluppata in due momenti. Entrambi i miei genitori sono artisti e spesso da bambina mi portavano a visitare musei. Una volta mi dissero che ci sono molte più opere d'arte nelle cantine che sui muri. Questo mi portò a chiedermi se c'era un modo di portare quelle opere alla luce in modo che più gente potesse vederle. Questo pensiero non mi lasciò mai. Mi dedicai a molte altre*

layers. There were massive technical hurtles to overcome.

FG: What's the relationship between the insubstantial and the material elements used in your work? What's the basic criteria you adopt when choosing subjects in your pieces?

IM: *All the subjects I choose must speak to me. I've been offered commissions of certain subjects that didn't move me and I was forced to turn them down. I get to know the subjects, historically and personally. They are real to me and tell me how they want to be presented in their new incarnation in my art. It is a kind of window for them to look out of and for us to look in at. I encapsulate their spirit into the layers of my work. I hope it doesn't sound too crazy, but I leave classical music going in my studio at night so they don't get lonely.*

FG: What's art for you? Historic characters, people coming from the past, are your favorites. Why?

IM: *Art is the communication of expression and emotion from object to viewer. Once the artist creates the object (artwork), he or she is released from this loop. That is why we can look at artwork from hundreds of years ago, have no idea who the artist was, and still be moved by the work. Art speaks across the centuries as easily as we speak to each other in person. My favorite characters are those of strong women. I often use queens and princesses in my work. They overcame great odds sometimes to do what they did. They inspire me and hopefully those who see them again in my work. I do use men as well, for the same reasons. François I is a fascinating character to me. He was a lover of art and brought the*

attività fino a che iniziai a lavorare per una galleria d'arte di Aspen. Il proprietario è ora mio marito da sedici anni. Lavorare in una galleria mi fece stare a contatto con tantissimi artisti e con l'Arte. La mia idea originaria continuò a frullarmi nel subconscio fino al 2005, quando affiorò in superficie. In un susseguirsi di sperimentazione giunsi alla mia attuale tecnica basata sulla stratificazione di immagini rinascimentali su strati trasparenti. C'erano enormi difficoltà tecniche da superare.

FG. Qual'è il rapporto fra l'inconsistenza e gli elementi materici che adotti nel tuo lavoro? Qual'è il criterio di base nella scelta dei soggetti delle tue opere?

I. *Tutti i soggetti che scelgo devono parlarmi. Mi sono state commissionate opere con soggetti che non mi emozionavano e sono stata costretta a rifiutare. Devo conoscere i soggetti, storicamente e personalmente. Per me sono reali e mi dicono come essi desiderano essere presentati nella loro nuova incarnazione tramite la mia Arte. Per loro è una specie di finestra da cui guardare l'esterno, e per noi in cui affacciarci. Io incapsulo il loro spirito negli strati del mio lavoro. Mi auguro questo non suoni un po' folle ma io di notte lascio accesa la musica classica nel mio studio, per non farli sentire soli.*

FG. Cos'è per te l'Arte? Personaggi storici, gente che viene dal passato sono i tuoi soggetti preferiti. Perché?

I. *L'Arte è la comunicazione di espressività ed emozione fra l'oggetto e lo spettatore. Una volta che l'artista crea l'oggetto (l'opera), lui o lei viene liberato. Ecco perché possiamo guardare un'opera d'arte di cento anni fa, non*

Mona Lisa to France. Many of my subjects are not well known, and I often use children as subjects. Their innocence appeals to me as does their strength.

FG: Would you please tell us something about your peculiar technique and your recent experimental work?

IM: *My technique is complex. I use multiple transparent layers to build a composite of images. In the spaces between, I place objects that speak to me such as music sheets, butterflies, fabric, toys, even coat hangers if the work calls for it. My most recent work is a slight departure from this. The back layer has the subject in black and white and the objects are layered in front of it. They are more haunting and subtle. Perhaps my favorite of this group is called "Memories of a Winter's Garden."*

Interview and translation by Federica Galetto, Editor WSF (Word Central Forum) Centro Sociale dell'Arte

Words Social Forum and Centro Sociale dell'Arte **is an Italian Blog dedicated to the creative arts. Ingrid was interviewed by Federica Galetto in August 2012 for the article. It is reprinted here in its entirety (excluding photographs and video).**

avere idea di chi sia l'artista, ed emozionarci ancora nel guardarla. L'Arte parla attraverso i secoli tanto facilmente quanto lo è per noi parlarci l'un l'altro di persona. I miei personaggi preferiti sono quelli di donne forti. Uso spesso figure di regine e principesse nel mio lavoro. Hanno dovuto superare enormi avversità talvolta, per fare ciò che hanno fatto. Mi ispirano e auspico ispirino anche coloro che le ritrovano nei miei quadri. Utilizzo anche figure maschili, per le stesse ragioni. François I è un personaggio che mi affascina. Era un amante dell'Arte e ha portato la Monna Lisa alla Francia. Molti dei miei soggetti non sono molto conosciuti e spesso ritraggo bambini. La loro innocenza mi attrae, così come la loro forza.

FG. Vuoi parlarci della tua peculiare tecnica artistica e del tuo recente lavoro sperimentale?

I. *La mia tecnica è complessa. Uso strati multipli trasparenti per costruire immagini composite. Tra gli spazi posiziono oggetti che mi parlano, come spartiti musicali, farfalle, tessuti, giocattoli, persino grucce se il lavoro lo richiede. Il mio lavoro più recente si discosta leggermente da questo. Lo strato posteriore ha il soggetto in bianco e nero e gli oggetti vengono stratificati davanti ad esso. In questo modo risultano più ammalianti e delicati. Forse, il mio preferito di questo gruppo è "Memories of a winter's garden.*

Intervista e traduzione di Federica Galetto, editore, WSF Centro Sociale dell'Arte

ILLUSION OF TIME II, 2012

REFLECTION, 2012

There is nothing to writing. All you do is sit down at a typewriter and bleed.

— ERNEST HEMINGWAY

DESTINY'S MEMORY, 2012

A CAMEO PERFORMANCE, 2012

THE ANGEL'S GUARDIAN, 2012

The only reason for time
is so that everything
doesn't happen at
once.

— ALBERT EINSTEIN

We all die. The goal isn't to live forever, the goal is to create something that will.

— Chuck Palahniuk, Novelist, b. 1961

The Traveler, 2012

116

All time is all time. It does not change. It does not lend itself to warnings or explanations. It simply is. Take it moment by moment, and you will find that we are all, as I've said before, bugs in amber.

— KURT VONNEGUT, *SLAUGHTERHOUSE V*

MEMORIES THROUGH TIME, 2012

2013

*H*ere's to the artists who have come before, the brave ones who ignored convention, broke down the walls and crashed the barriers that slowed the progress of art; to the ones who faced public ridicule and even risked their own lives for the realization of their vision; and here's to the artists of the future who will see what has never been seen and reveal it to all. For it is these men and women of profound courage who will one day redefine beauty itself and offer it to a world hungry for the sublime.

— INGRID & JAY MAGIDSON

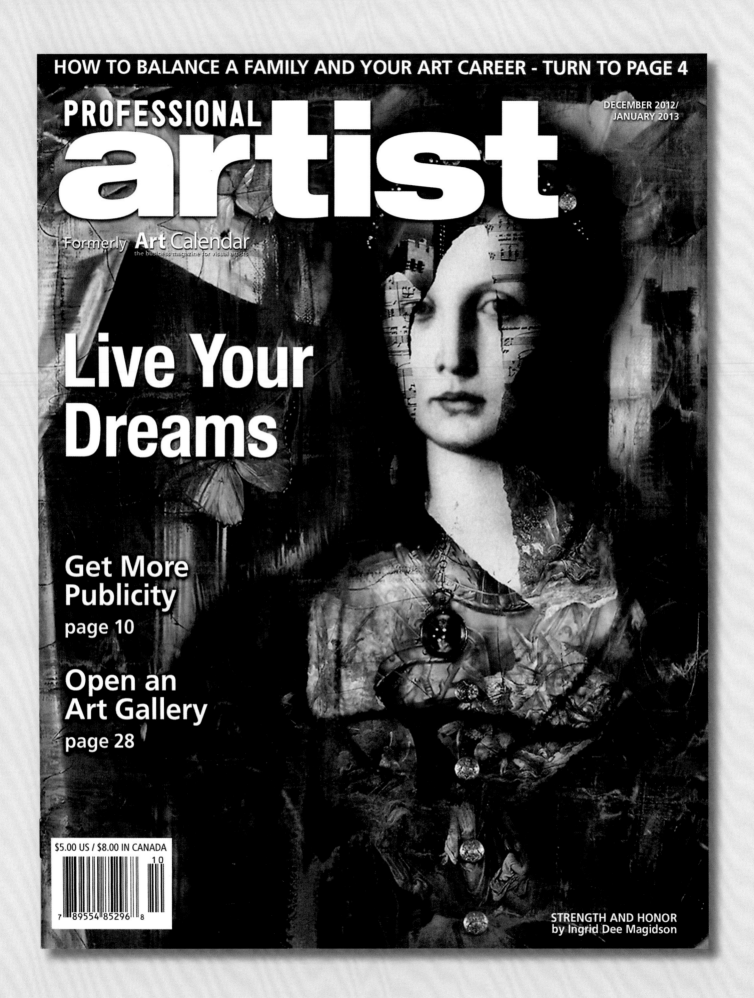

HOW TO BALANCE A FAMILY AND YOUR ART CAREER - TURN TO PAGE 4

PROFESSIONAL

artist

DECEMBER 2012/
JANUARY 2013

Formerly **Art** Calendar
the business magazine for visual artists

Live Your Dreams

Get More Publicity
page 10

Open an Art Gallery
page 28

STRENGTH AND HONOR
by Ingrid Dee Magidson

COVER ISSUE OF PROFESSIONAL ARTIST MAGAZINE, DECEMBER 2012/JANUARY 2013

Balancing a Family Life and a Creative Life

BY BRENDA HOPE ZAPPITELL

Magidson's family shows their support of her art by being very involved in her career.

Queen of Hearts, 2012, by Ingrid Dee Magidson
Layered mixed media, 35" x 32"

In Their Own Words

Ingrid Dee Magidson

Ingrid Dee Magidson (www.ingridmagidson.com) lives in Aspen, Colorado with her two children and husband. She has been one of the exhibited artists at the Hermitage Museum Foundation Benefit in New York for the last two years. She is represented by galleries in Aspen, Vail and Denver, Colorado, as well as Sante Fe, New Mexico. Her work also appeared in many publications, including Western Home Journal, Aspen Sojourner, Aspen Magazine, LUXE Magazine, Atlanta Homes & Lifestyles and Art and Living.

"My husband, Jay helps me with my framing and the construction of my works. He is also a writer. Our son, Teagan, is almost 12 years old; he loves football and skateboarding. Our 14-year-old daughter is named Isabella; she is so sweet and kind. We have a garden in our backyard and grow lots of fresh, yummy vegetables. We all love picking our food and preparing meals together in the kitchen.

"My husband and children love coming to my openings to support me - they are a part of all that I do. To see my work finally hanging in a gallery is not only a thrill for me but for them as well because they have been a part of the whole process (watching me work on each piece, helping me) - from the beginning to the end.

"I have found that taking those precious moments to meditate or going for a walk in my glorious surroundings (I live up in the mountains of Colorado) helps me keep me balanced within; then I am able to find that balance on the outside when taking care of my family and creating. I am very methodical, and with each new day, I prioritize. What is the most important thing that I need to complete first? Then I go from there. There will always be bumps in the road or unexpected distractions and daily interruptions; however, I remind myself everyday that I have been given a gift, and it is my purpose, it is my responsibility, and it is my obligation to fulfill it and to give it back. But mostly, I want to be an inspiration for my children and my husband.

"My studio is right next to our home, which is such a positive for me. I am able to step away from my studio and do chores too. It is also nice to have the time to prepare healthy meals instead of rushing it on the table. My husband now works with me, so we are both at home full-time. We have worked many years to get in this position. We are grateful it has worked out because when our kids get home from school they have both Mom and Dad to greet them."

They call me Mimì -
I don't know why.
I live all by myself
and I eat alone.
I don't often go to church,
but I like to pray.
I stay all alone
in my tiny white room,
I look at the roofs and the sky.
But when spring comes
the sun's first rays are mine.
April's first kiss is mine, is mine!
The sun's first rays are mine!
A rose blossoms in my vase,
I breathe its perfume, petal by petal.
So sweet is the flower's perfume.
But the flowers I make, alas,
the flowers I make, alas,
alas, have no scent.
What else can I say?

— Puccini, La Bohème, Act 1, 1896

Previous Page Left: Immortal Love, 2013
Previous Page Right: Passage Through Time, 2013

La Bohème, 2013

Cherish your visions and your dreams as they are the children of your soul, the blueprints of your ultimate achievements.

— Napoleon Hill

*W*hat we do in life,
echoes in eternity.

— Marcus Aurelius, *Meditations*, ca 175 A.D.

Echoes in Eternity, 2013

Let the end and the
beginning
Draw together into one!
Swifter than what's round thee spinning,
Thou thyself be flying on!
Thanks! the Muses' gracious giving
Makes the Imperishable thine;
In they breast the Substance living,
In thy soul the Form divine.

— GOETHE, FROM *STABILITY IN CHANGE*, 1839

INSIDE LOOKING OUT, 2013

To see a World in a Grain of Sand

And a Heaven in a Wild Flower

Hold Infinity in the palm of your hand

And Eternity in an hour

— WILLIAM BLAKE, *AUGURIES OF INNOCENCE*, 1803

BEYOND THE SHORES OF TIME, 2013

In This Sea of All, You Feel Alone

In this sea of All, you feel alone
A drop in an ocean of drops - separate, different
And you are dear one, different,
As different as the sun from the moon
But you are not alone
How could you be.

Your heart is known to the All,
It could not be otherwise.
And to know you - oh to know you,
A human enigma of compassion and pain
No, it is true - no man can truly know another
But beauty is in the trying.

Now close your eyes, and listen for the voice
Feel your skin tingle with the embrace of a million stars
The gentle breath on your heart
Warm and full of love
Brushes away the anguish and fear
Hold this gentle reminder close
And bathe again in the All.

— Jay Magidson

Behind the Mask, 2013

Catalogue of the Complete Works

2006 — 2013

O N the following pages, you will find all the finished works of Ingrid Dee Magidson from 2006 until May of 2013. The works are catalogued in order by the year they were created. The media of Magidson's works are constantly evolving, each is different and unique, as such, it is difficult to give a short description. For practical purposes, most works are listed simply as "layered paint, objects and acrylic." The majority of Magidson's works are layers of clear acrylic sheets with paint, collage, butterflies, and antique objects. These objects include, but are not limited to: watches, jewelry, book pages, ceramics, music sheets, brushes, silverware, chains, mirrors, fabric, shells, coral, coins, paper money, playing cards, antique photographs, knives, swords, doll furniture, miniature musical instruments, antique toys, music boxes, handmade paper, and a host of other materials.

Dimensions are given first in inches and second in centimeters in parenthesis. The sizes include the frame, as it is considered part of the art (the exception is for the earliest pieces in 2006 and 2007 where dimensions may only include the image size). The depth of each piece varies, but is never less than two inches. Many of the later pieces, "*Metamorphosis, 2010*," for example, are six or more inches deep.

CARNAL THOUGHTS, 2012

Love Will Return 2006
Collaboration with Eva Cellini
24 x 18 inches (61 x 46cm)
Layered paint and acrylic panel
Private Collection

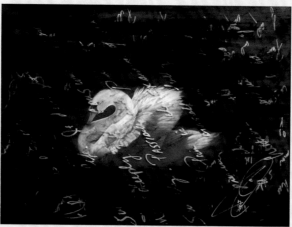

Art Sublime 2006
Collaboration with Eva Cellini
18 x 24 inches (46 x 61cm)
Layered paint and acrylic panel
Collection: John and Alicia Goldsmith

The Kiss 2006
35 x 29 inches (89 x 74cm)
Layered paint, objects & acrylic
Private Collection

Soar Away with Me 2006
35 x 29 inches (89 x 74cm)
Layered paint, objects & acrylic
Collection: Carter Tutwiler

Desire 2006
34 x 38 inches (86 x 97cm)
Layered paint, objects & acrylic
Private Collection

Missing You 2006
37 x 28 inches (94 x 71cm)
Layered paint and acrylic panel
Collection: Jeffrey & Linda Fine

Immortal Return 2006
35 x 29 inches (89 x 74cm)
Layered paint, objects & acrylic
Private Collection

Soar Away 2006
Collaboration with Eva Cellini
18 x 24 inches (46 x 61cm)
Layered paint and acrylic panel
Collection: Dotty Jacobs

Beginnings 2006
30 x 24 inches (76 x 61cm)
Layered paint, objects & acrylic
Collection: Sybil Hill

Melodic Memories of Joan of Arc 2007
53 x 44 inches (135 x 112cm)
Layered paint, objects & acrylic
Collection: Lisa and Gary Kallman

Voices in My Head 2007
53 x 41 inches (135 x 104cm)
Layered paint, objects & acrylic
Collection: Lester & Sue Smith

The Queen 2007
24 x 18 inches (61 x 46cm)
Layered paint, objects & acrylic
Collection: Lester & Sue Smith

The King 2007
24 x 18 inches (61 x 46cm)
Layered paint, objects & acrylic
Collection: Lester & Sue Smith

Temptation 2007
66 x 27 inches (168 x 69cm)
Layered paint, objects & acrylic
Collection: Penny Place & Bradley E. Place, Jr.

Isabella 2007
53 x 44 inches (135 x 112cm)
Layered paint, objects & acrylic
Collection: Isabella Magidson

Surrealism Lives in Me 2007
36 x 32 inches (91 x 81cm)
Layered paint, objects & acrylic
Collection: Philip & Joan Siwak

Homage to Eva 2007
53 x 43 inches (135 x 109cm)
Layered paint, objects & acrylic
Collection: John & Alicia Goldsmith

Dalíesque 2007
37 x 31 inches (94 x 79cm)
Layered paint, objects & acrylic
Collection: Penny Place &
Bradley E. Place, Jr.

Beyond the Clouds 2007
26 x 20 inches (66 x 51cm)
Layered paint, objects & acrylic
Collection: Marjorie Victor

Windows into your Soul 2007
26 x 22 inches (66 x 56cm)
Layered paint, objects & acrylic
Collection: Marjorie Victor

The Kiss 2007
72 x 38 inches (183 x 97cm)
Layered paint, objects & acrylic
Collection: Antonio Banderas
& Melonie Griffith

Desire 2007
22 x 36 inches (56 x 91cm)
Layered paint, objects & acrylic
Collection: Wewer Kohane

Madama Butterfly 2007
53 x 41 inches (135 x 104cm)
Layered paint, objects & acrylic
Collection: Steve & Elyse Blechman

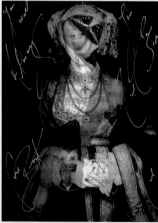

The Queen 2007
24 x 18 inches (51 x 46cm)
Layered paint, objects & acrylic
Collection: Colleen & Marcelo Ferreira

Searching for You 2007
48 x 38 inches (122 x 9cm)
Layered paint, objects & acrylic
Private Collection

Princess Hediyeh 2007
67 x 44 inches (170 x 112cm)
Layered paint, objects & acrylic
Private Collection

Distances Apart 2007
40 x 30 inches (102 x 76cm)
Layered paint, objects & acrylic
Collection: Lloyd & Betty Schermer

Queen of the House 2007
41 x 37 inches (104 x 94cm)
Layered paint, objects & acrylic
Collection: Lester & Sue Smith

Past Becomes Present 2008
54 x 34 inches (137 x 86cm)
Layered paint, objects & acrylic
Private Collection

Alive in Me 2007
30 x 24 inches (76 x 61cm)
Layered paint, objects & acrylic
Collection: Lester & Sue Smith

Release 2007
35 x 29 inches (89 x 74cm)
Layered paint, objects & acrylic
Collection: Robert & Debbie DeLeeuw

Inside Me You Live 2008
65 x 43 inches (165 x 109cm)
Layered paint, objects & acrylic
Private Collection

An Appetite for Life 2008
53 x 44 inches (135 x 112cm)
Layered paint, objects & acrylic
Collection: Deborah Sassoon & Daniel Gil

Birth of a Woman 2008
62 x 55 inches (157 x 140cm)
Layered paint, objects & acrylic
Private Collection

English Gothic 2008
53 x 63 inches (135 x 160cm)
Layered paint, objects & acrylic
Private Collection

Dust in the Wind 2008
68 x 53 inches (173 x 135cm)
Layered paint, objects & acrylic
Private Collection

Princess Dante 2008
30 x 16 inches (76 x 41cm)
Layered paint, objects & acrylic
Private Collection

Heirloom 2008
63 x 55 inches (160 x 140cm)
Layered paint, objects & acrylic
Private Collection

In Silence they Speak 2008
54 x 43 inches (137 x 109cm)
Layered paint, objects & acrylic
Private Collection

Friends Forever 2008
48 x 36 inches (122 x 91cm)
Layered paint, objects & acrylic
Collection: Kathryn & Richard Rabinow

Masquerade 2008
30 x 24 inches (76 x 61cm)
Layered paint, objects & acrylic
Private Collection

Oh So Very Velázquez 2008
60 x 53 inches (152 x 135cm)
Layered paint, objects & acrylic
Collection: The Lion Family

Budhalisque 2008
33 x 54 inches (84 x 137cm)
Layered paint, objects & acrylic
Collection: Gideon & Sarah Gartner

Tempt Me 2008
48 x 48 inches (122 x 122cm)
Layered paint, objects & acrylic
Private Collection

Once upon a Time 2008
47 x 40 inches (119 x 102cm)
Layered paint, objects & acrylic
Private Collection

Serene Beneath the Storm 2008
32 x 26 inches (81 x 66cm)
Layered paint, objects & acrylic
Collection: Marion Meyer

Princess Blue 2008
54 x 50 inches (137 x 127cm)
Layered paint, objects & acrylic
Collection: Tiffany Hunter

The Artist 2008
31 x 26 inches (79 x 66cm)
Layered paint, objects & acrylic
Collection: Paul Salcido

The King has Landed 2008
37 x 27 inches (94 x 69cm)
Layered paint, objects & acrylic
Private Collection

XOXO Mozart 2008
28 x 18 inches (71 x 46cm)
Layered paint, objects & acrylic
Private Collection

Queen of the House II 2008
42 x 38 inches (107 x 97cm)
Layered paint, objects & acrylic
Private Collection

Visionary 2008
52 x 40 inches (132 x 102cm)
Layered paint, objects & acrylic
Collection: Penny Place &
Bradley E. Place, Jr.

Temptress 2008
44 x 44 inches (112 x 112cm)
Layered paint, objects & acrylic
Collection: Marci & Ronnie Morgan

Always Connected 2008
63 x 42 inches (160 x 107cm)
Layered paint, objects & acrylic
Private Collection

Fairytale 2008
53 x 60 inches (135 x 152cm)
Layered paint, objects & acrylic
Private Collection

Inspirational Spirit 2008
52 x 45 inches (132 x 114cm)
Layered paint, objects & acrylic
Private Collection

Ti Amo da Vinci 2008
40 x 30 inches (102 x 76cm)
Layered paint, objects & acrylic
Collection: The Lion Family

Memories Within 2008
24 x 18 inches (61 x 46cm)
Layered paint, objects & acrylic
Donation: Basalt Schools

My da Vinci 2008
24 x 18 inches (61 x 46cm)
Layered paint, objects & acrylic
Private Collection

Long Live Louis 2008
54 x 40 inches (137 x 102cm)
Layered paint, objects & acrylic
Private Collection

Memories of a Time Forgotten 2008
53 x 44 inches (135 x 112cm)
Layered paint, objects & acrylic
Collection: Jackie Bezos

I Do Believe in Fairies 2008
36 x 22 inches (61 x 46cm)
Layered paint, objects & acrylic
Collection: Deborah Sassoon & Daniel Gil

Essence of Time 2008
65 x 50 inches (165 x 127cm)
Layered paint, objects & acrylic
Private Collection

The Past Lives Inside Me 2008
24 x 20 inches (61 x 51cm)
Layered paint, objects & acrylic
Collection: Traci & Alan Waserstein

Timeless Beauty 2008
36 x 28 inches (91 x 71cm)
Layered paint, objects & acrylic
Private Collection

The Angels Speak in Silence 2009
35 x 31 inches (89 x 79cm)
Layered paint, objects & acrylic
Donation: Aspen Deaf Camp

Unfolding Desires 2009
24 x 60 inches (61 x 152cm)
Layered paint, objects & acrylic
Collection: Dr. Wayne Yakes

Distant Shores Calling Me Back
2009, 69 x 42 inches (175 x 107cm)
Layered paint, objects & acrylic
Collection: Dr. Wayne Yakes

Mortal Desires 2009
35 x 30 inches (89 x 76cm)
Layered paint, objects & acrylic
Private Collection

Inspiration 2009
52 x 40 inches (132 x 102cm)
Layered paint, objects & acrylic
Collection: Hetta and Jesse Heath

Earthly Delights 2009
35 x 30 inches (89 x 76cm)
Layered paint, objects & acrylic
Collection: Dr. Mindy Nagle

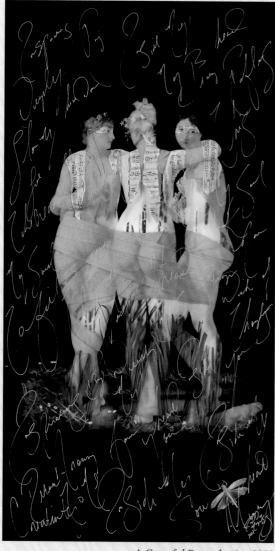

A Graceful Reawakening 2009
71 x 38 inches (180 x 97cm)
Layered paint, objects & acrylic
Collection: The Lion Family

Beyond the Horizon 2009
26 x 21 inches (66 x 53cm)
Layered paint, objects & acrylic
Collection: Buzz Peel

Dreams of a Woman 2009
30 x 48 inches (76 x 122cm)
Layered paint, objects & acrylic
Private Collection

Beethoven's Muse 2009
53 x 41 inches (135 x 104cm)
Layered paint, objects & acrylic
Collection: Penny Place &
Bradley E. Place, Jr.

Essence of Woman 2009
55 x 45 inches (140 x 114cm)
Layered paint, objects & acrylic
Collection: Deborah Sassoon & Daniel Gil

Inside Me You Live Always 2009
41 x 33 inches (104 x 84cm)
Layered paint, objects & acrylic
Collection: Jim & Bernice Kurtzner

Aspen Memories 2009
24 x 66 inches (61 x 168cm)
Layered paint, objects & acrylic
Collection: Vesna Hess

Always and Forever 2009
44 x 36 inches (112 x 91cm)
Layered paint, objects & acrylic
Collection: Dr. Wayne Yakes

Princess Ariel 2009
66 x 45 inches (168 x 114cm)
Layered paint, objects & acrylic
Collection: The Lion Family

Royal Fragments 2009
34 x 28 inches (86 x 71cm)
Layered paint, objects & acrylic
Private Collection

New Beginnings 2009
27 x 66 inches (69 x 168cm)
Layered paint, objects & acrylic
Collection: Sam & Cheryl Wyly

Sisters 2010
54 x 61 inches (137 x 155cm)
Layered paint, objects & acrylic
Collection: Dr. Wayne Yakes

Nature's Veil 2010
55 x 37 inches (140 x 94cm)
Layered paint, objects & acrylic
Collection: Mike & Paula Lisbe

Life's Echo 2010
42 x 36 inches (107 x 91cm)
Layered paint, objects & acrylic
Private Collection

Long Live the Queen 2010
48 x 46 inches (122 x 117cm)
Layered paint, objects & acrylic
Collection: Dr. Wayne Yakes

Tempt Me II 2010
36 x 36 inches (91 x 91cm)
Layered paint, objects & acrylic
Private Collection

Mother Nature 2010
70 x 31 inches (178 x 79cm)
Layered paint, objects & acrylic
Collection: Dr. Wayne Yakes

Awakening Desires 2010
67 x 32 inches (107 x 91cm)
Layered paint, objects & acrylic
Private Collection

Life's Treasures 2010
61 x 55 inches (155 x 140cm)
Layered paint, objects & acrylic
Collection: Dr. Wayne Yakes

Strength and Honor 2010
53 x 44 inches (135 x 112cm)
Layered paint, objects & acrylic
Collection: Penny Place & Bradley E. Place, Jr.

The Road Less Traveled 2010
48 x 42 inches (122 x 107cm)
Layered paint, objects & acrylic
Collection: Dr. Wayne Yakes

Gracefully Yours 2010
95 x 52 inches (241 x 132cm)
Layered paint, objects & acrylic
Collection: Dr. Wayne Yakes

Metamorphosis 2010
24 x 21 inches (61 x 53cm)
Layered paint, objects & acrylic
Collection: Jay Magidson

Honor 2010
27 x 21 inches (69 x 53cm)
Layered paint, objects & acrylic
Collection: Deborah Sassoon & Daniel Gil

The Illusion of Time 2010
35 x 25 inches (89 x 64cm)
Layered paint, objects & acrylic
Collection: Mark & Hanna Shaner

The Alchemist 2010
27 x 21 inches (69 x 53cm)
Layered paint, objects & acrylic
Private Collection

Positively Primitive 2010
40 x 34 inches (102 x 86cm)
Layered paint, objects & acrylic
Collection: Mark & Christina Dawson

Botticelli's Muse 2010
66 x 37 inches (168 x 94cm)
Layered paint & objects
Private Collection

Divinity 2010
61 x 39 inches (155 x 99cm)
Layered paint & objects
Private Collection

The Musician 2010
27 x 21 inches (69 x 53cm)
Layered paint, objects & acrylic
Collection: Dr. Wayne Yakes

Guardian Angel 2010
22 x 28 inches (56 x 71cm)
Layered paint, objects & acrylic
Private Collection

Always Calm Beneath 2010
61 x 51 inches (155 x 130cm)
Layered paint, objects & acrylic
Collection: Dr. Wayne Yakes

Night's Melody 2010
61 x 55 inches (155 x 140cm)
Layered paint, objects & acrylic
Private Collection

Another Season Past 2011
29 x 21 inches (74 x 53cm)
Layered paint, objects & acrylic
Private Collection

'Tis but a Brief Moment on this Mortal Stage 2011
28 x 23 inches (71 x 58cm)
Layered paint, objects & acrylic
Collection: Dr. Wayne Yakes

Layers of Discovery 2011
60 x 45 inches (152 x 114cm)
Layered paint, objects & acrylic
Collection: The Lion Family

*Your Words Awaken my
Sleeping Heart* 2011
41 x 30 inches (104 x 76cm)
Layered paint, objects & acrylic
Private Collection

Always Dear to My Heart 2011
33 x 48 inches (84 x 122cm)
Layered paint, objects & acrylic
Private Collection

Illumination 2011
55 x 40 inches (140 x 102cm)
Layered paint, objects & acrylic
Private Collection

Born to Reign 2011
37 x 29 inches (94 x 74cm)
Layered paint, objects & acrylic
Private Collection

The Warrior Within 2011
37 x 31 inches (94 x 79cm)
Layered paint, objects & acrylic
Private Collection

Seductress 2011
38 x 101 inches (97 x 257cm)
Layered paint, objects & acrylic
Private Collection

Love Will Find the Way 2011
53 x 44 inches (135 x 112cm)
Layered paint, objects & acrylic
Collection: The Lion Family

Nature Sublime 2011
33 x 29 inches (84 x 74cm)
Layered paint, objects & acrylic
Collection: Dara Mitchell

Our Eternity Begins Now 2011
53 x 38 inches (135 x 97cm)
Layered paint, objects & acrylic
Collection: Penny Place &
Bradley E. Place, Jr.

Peaceful Journey Brother 2011
56 x 47 inches (142 x 119cm)
Layered paint, objects & acrylic
Private Collection

The Guardian 2011
13 x 19 inches (33 x 48cm)
Layered paint, objects & acrylic
Private Collection

Paradise Within 2011
19 x 35 inches (48 x 89cm)
Layered paint, objects & acrylic
Collection: Penny Place & Bradley E. Place, Jr.

Two Divine 2011
53 x 60 inches (135 x 152cm)
Layered paint, objects & acrylic
Private Collection

Set Me Free 2011
29 x 24 inches (74 x 61cm)
Layered paint, objects & acrylic
Private Collection

The Woman Within 2011
53 x 41 inches (135 x 104cm)
Layered paint, objects & acrylic
Private Collection

An Appetite For Life II 2011
54 x 44 inches (137 x 112cm)
Layered paint, objects & acrylic
Private Collection

A Moment in Time 2011
60 x 46 inches (152 x 117cm)
Layered paint, objects & acrylic
Collection: Penny Place & Bradley E. Place, Jr.

Profoundly Yours 2011
19 x 13 inches (48 x 33cm)
Layered paint, objects & acrylic
Collection: Robert and Ellie Meyers

Queen of Hearts 2012
42 x 38 inches (107 x 97cm)
Layered paint, objects & acrylic
Collection: Penny Place &
Bradley E. Place, Jr.

Enchantress 2012
46 x 37 inches (117 x 94cm)
Layered paint, objects & acrylic
Collection: Penny Place & Bradley E. Place, Jr.

Enigma 2012
45 x 38 inches (114 x 97cm)
Layered paint, objects & acrylic
Private Collection

A Cameo Performance 2012
34 x 29 inches (86 x 74cm)
Layered paint, objects & wood
Collection of the Artist

Reverie 2012
45 x 34 inches (114 x 86cm)
Layered paint, objects & acrylic
Collection of the Artist

Salvation 2012
43 x 34 inches (109 x 86cm)
Layered paint, objects & acrylic
Private Collection

Return of the King 2012
45 x 29 inches (114 x 74cm)
Layered paint, objects & acrylic
Collection: Penny Place &
Bradley E. Place, Jr.

Time Waits for No One 2012
29 x 25 inches (74 x 64cm)
Layered paint, objects & acrylic
Collection: Jo Ellard

Whispered Memories 2012
30 x 23 inches (75 x 58cm)
Layered paint, objects & acrylic
Collection of the Artist

Einstein's Muse 2012
34 x 33 inches (86 x 84cm)
Layered paint, objects & wood
Collection of the Artist

Memoirs 2012
43 x 38 inches (109 x 97cm)
Layered paint, objects & acrylic
Collection: Barb Preston

The Butterfly Effect 2012
31 x 26 inches (79 x 66cm)
Layered paint, objects & acrylic
Private Collection

Destiny's Memory 2012
53 x 43 inches (135 x 109cm)
Layered paint, objects & acrylic
Collection: Jo Ellard

Return of Pegasus 2012
35 x 48 inches (89 x 122cm)
Layered paint, objects & acrylic
Collection: Hotel Alpina Gstaad

The Madness of the Muses 2012
50 x 31 inches (127 x 79cm)
Layered paint, objects & acrylic
Private Collection

Homage to the King 2012
23 x 19 inches (58 x 48cm)
Layered paint, objects & wood
Collection of the Artist

The Illusion of the Time II 2012
36 x 24 inches (66 x 61cm)
Layered paint, objects & acrylic
Collection: Don & Sara Nelson

Memories of a Winter's Garden 2012
49 x 35 inches (124 x 89cm)
Layered paint, objects & wood
Collection: Elaine & Dan Berg

The Winds of Time 2012
38 x 23 inches (97 x 58cm)
Layered paint, objects & wood
Collection: Wayne & Leslie Pathman

Queen of Masquerade 2012
60 x 35 inches (152 x 89cm)
Layered paint, objects & wood
Collection: Jo Ellard

The Family 2012
4 x 6 inches (10 x 15cm)
Layered paint, objects & acrylic
Collection of the Artist

Lost in a Dream 2012
29 x 45 inches (74 x 114cm)
Layered paint, objects & wood
Collection of the Artist

King of Renaissance 2012
60 x 35 inches (152 x 89cm)
Layered paint, objects & wood
Collection of the Artist

The Eminence of Time 2012
61 x 38 inches (155 x 97cm)
Layered paint, objects & acrylic
Collection of the Artist

Lady Di 2012
5 x 4 inches (13 x 10cm)
Layered paint, objects & acrylic
Collection: David & Diane Magidson

King David 2012
5 x 4 inches (13 x 10cm)
Layered paint, objects & acrylic
Collection: David & Diane Magidson

Bianca 2012
5 x 4 inches (13 x 10cm)
Layered paint, objects & acrylic
Collection: Don & Sara Nelson

The Oracle 2012
20 x 15 inches (51 x 39cm)
Layered paint, objects & acrylic
Collection: Jay Magidson

Together We'll Make History 2012
47 x 36 inches (119 x 91cm)
Layered paint, objects & acrylic
Collection: Brooke & James Levy

Into the Eternal Sea 2012
37 x 26 inches (94 x 66cm)
Layered paint, objects & acrylic
Collection of the Artist

Queen Elaine 2012
4 x 11 inches (10 x 28cm)
Layered paint, objects & acrylic
Collection: Elaine Joyce Hill

Reflection 2012
43 x 33 inches (109 x 84cm)
Layered paint, objects & acrylic
Collection: Tsukanov Family Foundation, London

The Creator 2012
50 x 70 inches (127 x 178cm)
Layered paint, objects & acrylic
Private Collection

The World is Your Oyster 2012
80 x 56 inches (203 x 142cm)
Layered paint, objects & acrylic
Collection: Elaine & Dan Berg

Carnal Thoughts 2012
22 x 17 inches (56 x 43cm)
Layered paint, objects & wood
Collection: Eva Cellini

My Vision Becomes my Release 2012
28 x 24 inches (71 x 61cm)
Layered paint, objects & acrylic
Collection: Dana Banovitz

The Traveler 2012
31 x 25 inches (79 x 64cm)
Layered paint, objects & acrylic
Collection of the Artist

The Gilded Cage 2012
55 x 43 inches (140 x 109cm)
Layered paint, objects & wood
Collection: Penny Place & Bradley E. Place, Jr.

The Angels' Guardian 2012
38 x 30 inches (97 x 76cm)
Layered paint, objects & acrylic
Private Collection

Gaia 2012
26 x 22 inches (66 x 56cm)
Layered paint, objects & acrylic
Collection: Penny Place &
Bradley E. Place, Jr.

Don't Bluff Me 2012
37 x 32 inches (94 x 81cm)
Layered paint, objects & acrylic
Collection of the Artist

Memories Through Time 2012
60 x 50 inches (152 x 127cm)
Layered paint, objects & acrylic
Collection of the Artist

Ode to Joy 2012
47 x 32 inches (119 x 81cm)
Layered paint, objects & acrylic
Private Collection

Inside Looking Out 2013
75 x 44 inches (188 x 109cm)
Layered paint, objects & acrylic
Collection of the Artist

La Bohème 2013
50 x 50 inches (127 x 127cm)
Layered paint, objects & acrylic
Collection of the Artist

Cherished Memories of Cornell's Last Muse 2013
51 x 34 inches (130 x 86cm)
Layered paint, objects & acrylic
Collection of the Artist

Behind the Mask 2013
73 x 43 inches (185 x 109cm)
Layered paint, objects & acrylic
Collection of the Artist

Bianca's Diary 2013
32 x 24 inches (81 x 61cm)
Layered paint, objects & acrylic
Collection: Shirley Orsak

Beyond the Shores of Time 2013
61 x 36 inches (155 x 91cm)
Layered paint, objects & acrylic
Collection of the Artist

Immortal Love 2013
64 x 29 inches (163 x 74cm)
Layered paint, objects & acrylic
Collection of the Artist

The Ebb of Time 2013
43 x 34 inches (109 x 86cm)
Layered paint, objects & acrylic
Collection of the Artist

Homage to Duchamp 2013
9 x 8 inches (23 x 20cm)
Layered paint, objects & acrylic
Collection of the Artist

Echoes in Eternity 2013
55 x 37 inches (140 x 94cm)
Layered paint, objects & acrylic
Collection of the Artist

Passage Through Time 2013
50 x 41 inches (127 x 104cm)
Layered paint, objects & acrylic
Collection of the Artist

Ingrid Dee Magidson
Curriculum Vitæ

AMERICAN, B. 1965
LIVES & WORKS IN CARBONDALE, CO

SELECTED COLLECTIONS

ALPINA HOTEL, GSTAAD, SWITZERLAND

DARA MITCHELL, NYC

TSUKONOV FAMILY FOUNDATION, LONDON

MARY BUCKSBAUM SCANLAN, ASPEN, CO

SAM AND CHERYL WYLY, ASPEN, CO; DALLAS, TX

ANTONIO BANDERAS AND MELANIE GRIFFITH, NYC

JACKIE BEZOS, SEATTLE, WA

GIDEON AND SARAH GARTNER, NYC

LESTER AND SUE SMITH, HOUSTON, TX

ELAINE AND DAN BERG

LLOYD AND BETTY SCHERMER, ASPEN, CO/TUCSON, AZ

WAYNE AND LESLIE PATHMAN, MIAMI, FL/ASPEN, CO

JOHN AND ALICIA GOLDSMITH, LOS ANGELES, CA

MARJORIE VICTOR, LOS ANGELES, CA

CARTER TUTWILER, HANA, HI

ROBERT AND DEBBIE DeLEEUW, CHICAGO, IL

MARION MEYER, LAGUNA BEACH, CA

METROPOLIS AGENCY, LOS ANGELES, CA

KATHRYN AND RICHARD RABINOW, HOUSTON, TX

THE MORGAN GROUP, CARLSBAD, CA

PENNY PLACE & BRADLEY E. PLACE, JR., DENVER, CO

RED BARRIS, LOS ANGELES, CA

LA PIETRA CUCINA, ATLANTA, GA

NICOLE FOLGER, SYDNEY, AUSTRALIA

DR. WAYNE YAKES, DENVER, CO

ENCHANTRESS, 2012

Selected Exhibitions

August 3, 2013, Solo Exhibition: Forré Fine Art,
 Aspen, CO

July 25, 2013 Art Southampton, Southampton, NY

February 13-17, 2013, Art Wynwood, Miami, FL

December 7-January 2, 2013, Unix Fine Art, Miami, FL

Dec 7-9, 2012, Art Miami, Unix Fine Art, Miami, FL

December 4, 2012, Solo Exhibition: Pathman
 Residence, Miami Beach, FL

November 8, 2012, Hermitage Museum Foundation;
 Philips de Pury, NYC

July 2012, Solo Exhibition: Galerie Züger, Vail, CO

November 4, 2011, Hermitage Museum Foundation;
 Sotheby's, NYC

May 2011, Solo Exhibition, Masters Gallery,
 Greenwood Village, CO

Aug 2011, Anderson Ranch Art Center, Snowmass, CO

Feb 2011, Solo Exhibition: Galerie Züger, Vail, CO

June 2010 Singleton-Biss Museum of Fine Art,
 Santa Fe, NM

May 20, 2010 Solo Exhibition: Master's Gallery,
 Greenwood Village, CO

March 12, 2010 Solo Exhibition: David Floria
 Gallery, Aspen, CO

December 3, 2009 Solo Exhibition: Marion Meyer
 Contemporary Art, Laguna Beach, CA

November 5, 2009, Solo Exhibition: Marion Meyer
 Contemporary Art, Laguna Beach, CA

Aug 2009, Anderson Ranch Art Center, Snowmass, CO

October 2009, Bill Clinton Fund Raising Event,
 Bill Lowe Gallery, Atlanta, GA

Aug 2008, Anderson Ranch Art Center, Snowmass, CO

May 1, 2008 Solo Exhibition: Marion Meyer
 Contemporary Art, Laguna Beach, CA

Jan 16 - Feb 15, 2009, Bill Lowe Gallery, Atlanta, GA

July 7, 2007, Solo Exhibition: Magidson Fine Art,
 Aspen, CO

Selected Bibliography

Miroir Magazine, Primavera, Cover & Article,
    April, 2013

Professional Artist, Cover & Article, Dec 2012/Jan 2013

Centro Sociale dell'Arte, Social Words Forum,
    September 2012

Western Home Journal, Aspen, Winter 2012

Art, Vail Valley Gallery Guide, Cover & Article
    Spring, 2011

ArtScene, December, 2009, Exhibition Review

Anderson Ranch Art Center, 2009, 2011 catalogue

LUXE Magazine, January 2009

Atlanta Homes & Lifestyles, January 2009

Art and Living Magazine, Los Angeles, May 2008

Laguna Beach Independent, June 2008

Laguna Beach Alliance for the Arts, Cover,
    Summer 2008

Anderson Ranch Art Center, 2008 catalogue

The Aspen Times, Cover and Article July, 7, 2007

Aspen Sojourner, Summer 2006

Donation & Nonprofit Recipients

Hermitage Museum Foundation, NYC

The Aspen Art Museum, Aspen, CO

Anderson Ranch, Snowmass, CO

Aspen Deaf Camp, Snowmass, CO

Voices of Tomorrow Foundation, Aspen, CO

Basalt Kids, Basalt, CO

Film

2011, *Windows Through Time*, 21 min, The Reid Effect
(2012 Silver Telly Award for Best Documentary)

Online

www.IngridMagidson.com

blog.IngridMagidson.com

www.youtube.com/user/Ingriddeemagidson

www.facebook.com/ingrid.magidson

twitter.com/ingridmagidson

pinterest.com/magidson/

From Left to Right: Ingrid with gallery owner, Marion Meyer, 2008 exhibition in Laguna Beach; Jay & Ingrid; Ingrid & Hedy; Sybil & Ingrid; Ingrid with collectors: Deborah Sassoon & Daniel Gil and Marion Meyer at her 2009 exhibition; Sybil & daughter Brigette; Isabella, Ingrid, Teagan & Jay at David Floria Gallery and exhibition, 2010; Ingrid; Ingrid, Alan Fletcher, director of Aspen Music Festival and gallery owner, David Floria; Collectors: Bernice Kurtzner and Buzz Peel with Ingrid at the Laguna Beach reception; Ann Korologos, owner of Ann Korologos Gallery in Basalt, CO with Jay & Ingrid; Twins: Sybil & Ingrid at David Floria Gallery opening, 2010.

From Left to Right, Top to Bottom: Ingrid with gallery owner, Bonnie Züger at her gallery opening in Denver, 2010; Master's Gallery opening reception, 2010; Ingrid with *Gracefully Yours;* collectors, Brad & Penny Place with Ingrid; Ingrid with gallery owner, Paul Züger; collector, Dr. Wayne Yakes with Ingrid at Masters Gallery reception, Denver, 2010; Collectors: Dr. Wayne Yakes, Brad Place with Ingrid; gallery owners, Paul & Bonnie Züger; Jay, Isabella, Ingrid & Teagan at the Galerie Züger opening in Vail, 2011; Ingrid; Ingrid & Isabella at Vail opening, 2011; Ingrid with Galerie Züger staff: Rob & Joyce and gallery director, Rayla Kundolf.

Ingrid & Teagan, Galerie Züger Vail, 2011; Magidson Family; Ingrid; Unix Gallery owners: Daniela Mercuri, Alex Cesaria with Andrea Pasin, Art Miami, 2012; gallery owner, Ania Forré & Ingrid in her studio, 2012; Ingrid & mom, Elaine Hill, Vail opening, 2011; Jay & Ingrid opening night, Art Basil/Miami, 2012; Jay & Ingrid, Art Miami, 2012; gallery owner, Andi Potampkin & Madison Pathman at Ingrid's exhibition Miami, 2012; Leslie Pathman & Ingrid; Ingrid with *Reflection*, Hermitage Museum FND Benefit, Philips de Pury, NYC, 2012; Brad Place, Margarita Kelner, Ingrid & *A Moment in Time*, Hermitage Museum FND Benefit, Sotheby's, NY, 2011; Ingrid before the auction.

Collector, Dara Mitchell & Ingrid, NYC, 2012; Ingrid, Sybil, Jay & artist Eva Cellini at her exhibition, 2008; Rob Reid Effect filming Ingrid for *Window's Through Time,* documentary on Ingrid's work, 2010; Rob Reid & assistant filming; Jay with *Gracefully Yours* before framing; Isabella in Ingrid's Studio, 2008; Ingrid in her studio doing a video update, 2013; Mary McClure, David Floria Gallery opening, 2010; Isabella in front of her namesake artwork, 2007; Collector, Alicia Goldsmith, daughter Gillian & Ingrid; Teagan & Isabella goofing at a photoshoot, 2008

From Left to Right, Top to Bottom: Collector, Brad Place; Ingrid & Jay on the way to Telluride, CO; Melton (dad/grandpa) Magidson with Isabella as a baby; Isabella, Ingrid, Teagan; Teagan, first visit to NYC, 2012; Jay, Isabella & Teagan; Ingrid, Isabella & Teagan, Hunter Creek, Aspen; Jay & Teagan, X-Games, Aspen, CO; Magidson Family, Maroon Bells, Aspen, CO; Teagan; silly Isabella & Teagan; Jay & Ingrid's wedding, June 30, 1996; Bernice Kurtzner (grandma B), Ingrid and Teagan; Teagan & Isabella being silly (again); Jay, Isabella, Teagan and Trigger at Maroon Bells, Aspen, CO.

Cousin Brigette, Isabella & Teagan; Teagan, Museum of Modern Art, NYC; Isabella & Teagan, Mardi Gras; Ingrid & Isabella in Florida; Ingrid, Teagan & Isabella, birthday in Vail; Ingrid, Teagan & Isabella, Denver Aquarium; Ingrid & Teagan, fourth birthday; Jay, Isabella & Teagan, Arches, Utah; Magidson Family with Gessocat, Christmas 2001; Isabella posing; Teagan & Ingrid Grand Central Station, NYC; Jay & Teagan, Butterfly Museum, Boulder, CO; Irving Hill (Grandpa), Teagan, Isabella & Ingrid; Jay, Teagan, Ingrid & Eva Cellini, NJ; Magidson Family, biking; Magidson Family, Little Cayman, Father's Day, 2012; Magidson Family, Carbondale, Thanksgiving, 2011

Acknowledgements

Here's to all those people who have crossed my path during this journey of life, I am grateful to you for sharing your love and light with me, for I would not be who I am if I had not met you along the way. I thank God for your presence in my life. First, thank you Jay, my husband, my partner in life and work, my friend and lover. You've stood by me through thick and thin, always believing in me and my work. I couldn't do it without you. Isabella and Teagan, my glorious angels, you are my center, my connection to the earth and my heart. Thank you mom and dad for exposing me to art and creativity and loving me. Sybil, my dearest twin, you inspire me as we share our gifts with the world. I love you! Eva Cellini, for your never-ending inspiration and love. Brad and Penny for your passionate support and belief in my work. Jill, for your love and laughter. Kendra, you are a godsend, thank you for being there at those odd hours. Mary, together we sang "The Hills Are Alive..." and you became my lifelong friend. Alicia - my beautiful and dear friend, we are always connected, you are a gift to me. To my brothers, Peter and Jeff thank you for being a part of my journey. Bernice Kurtzner (grandma, mom) for your unconditional love. My dear Iryna, you are an angel and a blessing in our lives. I'd have to add another book to list all the ways the rest of you, my dear friends and family, have helped and inspired me. Instead I will simply say thank you, knowing that you know why and how much: Melton Magidson, Steve & Ariel Magidson, David Magidson and family, Anna & Jamie Marx, Beth & Kay, Eva & Eric Pekkala, Lloyd & Betty Schermer, Carter Tutwiler, Craig O'Brian, Paul & Bonnie Züger and the staff of the Masters and Züger Galleries, Marion Meyer, David & Kim Floria, Ania Forré and the staff of the Forré Gallery, Alex Cesaria & Daniela Mercuri, Lester & Sue Smith, Bruce & Robin Lion, Deborah Sassoon & Daniel Gil, Tom & Ann Korologos, Dr. & Mrs. Wayne Yakes, Wayne & Leslie Pathman, Dara Mitchell, Don & Sara Nelson, Charles Abbott & Digital Arts Aspen, Katie Hunsberger, Stewart Oxenhorn, Mark Kelner, Deepak & Gayatri. And a special thank you to the Shoshoni Ashram and Yoga Retreat - you saved, then changed my life.